This book is intended to offer an introduction to some major themes in literacy education. Literacy has become an important issue both in the UK and internationally, and this book aims to inform discussions while assisting teachers to reflect on their work as literacy teachers. Literacy is important from the earliest years through all the years of formal education, and so this book covers work with students in the full range of schooling, and in a number of different subject areas.

Topics covered include: the nature and use of texts; the reading positions that are constructed in texts and their ideological implications; the ways in which written texts change as students grow older; moving from the early years through to secondary education; and the implications of IT for literacy teaching.

Frances Christie is Foundation Professor of Language and Literacy Education at the University of Melbourne. **Ray Misson** is Senior Lecturer in Language and Literacy Education and Associate Dean, Preservice Programs at the University of Melbourne.

Literacy and Schooling

Edited by Frances Christie
and Ray Misson

London and New York

First published
1998 by Routledge
11 New Fetter Lane, London EC4P 4EE

Simultaneously published in the USA and Canada
by Routledge
29 West 35th Street, New York, NY 10001

Typeset in Sabon by Routledge
Printed and bound in Great Britain by TJ International Ltd,
Padstow, Cornwall

British Library Cataloguing in Publication Data
A catalogue record for this book is available from the British
Library

Library of Congress Cataloguing in Publication Data
Literacy and schooling/edited by Frances Christie and Ray Misson.
Includes bibliographical references and index.
1. Literacy – Great Britain. 2. Language arts – Great Britain.
3. Reading – Great Britain. I. Christie, Frances. II. Misson, Ray.
LC156.L55   1998
97–47649
302.2'244'0941–dc21   CIP

ISBN 0–415–17017–6 (hbk)
ISBN 0–415–17018–4 (pbk)

Contents

Illustrations

Figures

Tables

Contributors

Frances Christie is Foundation Professor of Language and Literacy Education at the University of Melbourne.

Michele Knobel is a Lecturer in Language and Literacy Education at the Queensland University of Technology.

Colin Lankshear is Professor and Research Director in the School of Language and Literacy Education, Queensland University of Technology.

Mary Macken-Horarik is a Lecturer in Language and Literacy Education at the University of Technology, Sydney.

Ray Misson is a Senior Lecturer in Language and Literacy Education and Associate Dean, Preservice Programs at the University of Melbourne.

Wendy Morgan is a Senior Lecturer in Language and Literacy Education at the Queensland University of Technology.

Geoff Williams is a Senior Lecturer in the Department of English at the University of Sydney.

Acknowledgements

The editors and contributors to this book wish to thank the following: Julie Vivas and Omnibus Books for permission to print extracts from the children's novel *I Went Walking*; Margaret Harris, journalist, for permission to print an article 'Doctors find cure for cystic fibrosis', which originally appeared in *The Sun Herald* on 2 July 1989.

Framing the issues in literacy education

Frances Christie and Ray Misson

The demands made on literacy, and so on literacy teachers, are always changing, and the range of those demands is expanding in crucial ways as we approach the millennium. It therefore seems timely to gather together some examples of work in the area of literacy that suggest the important issues confronting literacy teaching at the moment, and the kinds of answers that are being found in best research-based practice.

Literacy is a complex field. Many of the terms involved, such as 'literacy' itself, have many meanings and are used in a wide variety of literal and metaphorical ways. There are also many different strands within literacy teaching, not necessarily conflicting, and different frameworks within which it is conceptualised. Before turning to the individual contributions to this volume, it will be useful to discuss and attempt to clarify some of these complexities.

The concept of literacy

Until very recent times, the custom in educational theory and discussion was to talk of the teaching of reading and writing, rather than the teaching of literacy. Reading and writing were seen as separate skills. Time-honoured practice, going back some centuries, required that students learn to read first, moving on to learn writing much later on. In practice, in the nineteenth century and even in the early years of this century, many educational programmes for children, particularly at the elementary level, concentrated on the teaching of reading only, requiring no more than that the children also learned to pen their names. There was a sense in which, in much educational practice, reading was often seen as the more significant skill. Writing gained more significance for those students fortunate to stay on at school for the secondary years.

From the fifteenth century on, a 'literate person' has been one who was acquainted with letters or with literature. The juxtaposition of the two terms is interesting: to be familiar with literature, one needed to know the alphabet, and this was a measure of one's status as an educated person.

One who was 'illiterate' was necessarily ignorant of letters, and hence also of literature. But though the terms 'literate' and 'illiterate' were known and in use for several centuries, the term 'literacy' was not widely used. Teaching was understood to be about reading and writing, where these were seen as somewhat separate skills. Teacher education dates from the second half of the nineteenth century, and the first teacher training programmes in the English-speaking world attached a great deal of importance to preparing their trainee teachers for instructing the young in their letters. Instruction in one's letters for the greater majority of children in the elementary schools of the nineteenth century was about learning to recognise the alphabet, to be able to read improving works, including religious tracts, and perhaps to write one's name. But the term 'literacy' was not a term much in use, nor was it widely used in educational discussions for much of the first half of this century.

After the second world war, a great many former colonies around the world became newly launched independent nations, and a priority for such nations very early on was to provide adequate educational opportunity for their children. Education was closely linked to the building of economic security. Bodies like the United Nations, and related agencies such as UNICEF and UNESCO have, in the postwar period, devoted large amounts of resources to educational provision in the developing countries. After the 1960s, international agencies began to develop programmes in 'functional literacy' – a term intended to capture a sense of a basic competence in reading and writing of a kind held to be sufficient for fostering efficient and informed workers.

The year 1990 was declared the International Literacy Year (ILY), sponsored by the United Nations. The fact that such a year was instituted speaks in itself for the worldwide significance that had come to be attached to possession of literacy. The ILY led to the development of many literacy programmes in the developing world, but it also had an impact in developed countries such as the UK, Australia and the USA, where additional money was spent on developing new policies to promote literacy.

Stimulated in part by initiatives like the ILY, the English-speaking countries have increasingly come to use the term 'literacy', both in official policy statements prepared by governments and in a great deal of educational theorising.

To take the issue of official government policy first, it is notable that during the election that saw Blair lead the British Labour Party into office in 1997, he and his colleagues made educational provision, including provision of literacy programmes, a major electioneering theme. A Literacy Taskforce, appointed while the party was still in opposition, went to work on developing policies, and a new government White Paper, launched in 1997, stressed the importance of literacy teaching as a means of bringing about a renewal of purpose and commitment in British schools. In Australia, the Liberal Party came to office in 1996, and it too began to develop a range of policies intended to enhance the teaching of literacy in Australian schools. These included adoption of so-called 'literacy benchmarks' for gauging children's performance at different levels of schooling. Politicians of all political parties regularly allude to the importance of literacy, often linking success in it to the development of enhanced national prosperity.

Often, in fact, the apparent connection suggested between literacy and economic well-being is too simple. Possession of literacy will not in itself guarantee any individual the certainty of work, and it is naive to suggest that it will. However, it is also true that in the contemporary world, any individual without literacy will probably be unemployed or, at best, obliged to take up one of the few, probably poorly paid, remaining occupations available that don't require literacy. The latter observation is important for a number of reasons, not least that it points to the profound social changes brought about this century because of the extension of literacy.

Literacy has genuinely changed the world, and it continues to change it in ways about which we are often not even very conscious. The sheer volume of printed materials available now in the world is of a size greater than at any time in human history. More and more information, knowledge, ideas, advice, literature and entertainment are available in the printed word. Add to this the awesome impact of information technology, the fact that we often don't even use the printed word at all these days, instead relying on digital means, and we begin to understand the remarkable changes to literacy in the modern world. The work of modern businesses, governments, educational systems, legal systems, health systems, and so on, is made possible because of our capacity to generate information in writing and to communicate it at speed both within our own communities, and around the world.

It is because of the profound changes in literacy this century, and because of the exciting possibilities many scholars see in discussing literacy and its role in pedagogy, that we have seen the upsurge in theorising about it, alluded to above. Literacy has proved to be a fertile field for a great deal of educational theory, leading to the publication of many books and journal articles about literacy, ways to define it, and ways to teach it. Many theorists have resisted notions of 'functional literacy', arguing instead for models of literacy that are in some sense more empowering of the individual. Hence the term 'critical literacy', associated with writers such as Giroux, Luke, Lankshear and Fairclough. This is a term we will look at in a little more detail below.

A number of other, increasingly metaphorical ways of using the term 'literacy' have appeared. When E. D. Hirsch, for example, writes about 'cultural literacy', he is referring to knowledge of particular valued cultural 'facts' (names of authors, names of places, basic philosophical terminology, etc.) that might be referred to in a text, and which writers should be able to expect the normally 'cultured' person to know. For his project of cultural literacy, these snippets of knowledge are seen almost as the equivalent of the letters in the alphabet in older notions of learning how to read, and schools are castigated for not having taught them to students. Others write of 'visual literacy', drawing attention to the facts (i) that the act of responding to and interpreting images of various kinds is itself a skill requiring tuition and cultivation, and (ii) that in a world of increasingly easy access to computers, students will all learn to create texts that exploit and blend the resources of verbal texts and images of many kinds. Other writers write of 'computer literacy', which is of course increasingly significant, given the growing impact of computers in schools, homes and workplaces, and the consequent need for most people nowadays to be able to understand and work with computer technology.

Overall, we would argue that the increasing frequency with which teachers and educational theorists have come to use the term 'literacy' in the second half of this century is both useful and important. It is a measure of the fact that they have come to see reading and writing as so intimately interrelated that we cannot understand the one without the other. Reading and writing are not discrete, isolable skills. Theorists and teachers alike have come to realise increasingly that the most successful teaching programmes will encourage students to move freely between reading and writing. The most successful reader is often also the most successful writer, and the best teaching programmes will guide students to draw on their skills in the one to develop their skills in the other. No doubt in any teaching programme there will be points at which teachers and students will need to give greater emphasis to either reading or writing, but it will be development of proficiency in both which is the measure of educational success.

Literacy truly is a remarkable phenomenon. Like oral language as well, we can think of literacy as a technology, as a kind of tool humans have learned to exploit in order to serve their many purposes. The advent of literacy many centuries ago began to change the very nature of the human societies that used it, opening new ways of constructing and ordering information, and making possible the development of new discoveries of many kinds. Literacy both changes the nature of human societies and is changed by them. As we fast approach the twenty-first century, it is already clear that literacy is again rapidly changing, bringing about other changes in the ways we construct and order information. In the process literacy change will no doubt open the way to many as yet unimagined means of constructing and communicating information. Whether all the changes made possible will be desirable is itself a very important question. So important is this question that it requires that teachers do all they can to develop students able to question, and able to discriminate between those developments worth preserving and those that should be challenged.

In a world in which change is commonplace, and rapid change apparently the norm, it is clear that educational systems will need to assist students of the future to anticipate and deal with change. Among the many possible strategies needed to assist students to prepare will be the development of programmes that will equip them to understand literacy, its relationship to oral language, its infinite capacity for adaptation to make new meanings, and its significance as a social phenomenon. This last notion is particularly significant and deserves consideration in itself.

Literacy as a social phenomenon

If there is one major idea that colours the field of literacy in the late 1990s, it is that all language and literacy are social. In many ways, there is nothing new about this. Language is a social phenomenon through and through and has always been recognised as such. It obviously developed from a need to communicate, which necessarily presupposes some primitive social interactions. Language is a *sine qua non* of any human society. One would not want to deny our apelike ancestors, gibbering and gesturing in their caves, the dignity of having formed communities, but one cannot conceive of any genuinely human society that is not based on language. Language gives the ability to make absent things present for contemplation and discussion, the ability to manipulate ideas in subtle ways. It gives the capacity to execute communal actions on a large and complex scale that requires the means to plan, divide up responsibilities and monitor progress.

Literacy, like oral language, has always been seen as concerned with community too. Through the power of literacy to reach across time and space, society is all the more powerfully maintained and developed: innovation can be more easily shared, trade transactions can be recorded, a huge range of knowledge can be accessed, laws more easily enforced. Literacy is, rather more than language in general, particularly concerned with the reproduction of a society that is suitably skilled and/or properly moral.

Given all this, it may seem strange to insist that the distinctively new feature of literacy education in the past decade or so is a recognition of the social nature of language and literacy. The difference, of course, lies in the kind of social theory being used to frame the phenomenon. Sociology began to influence linguistic research strongly from the 1960s, providing a focus on such things as the importance of language in the building of social life, its role in the development of children as social beings, and the significance of language in institutions of socialisation such as schools. Social theorists as diverse as Berger and Luckmann, Mary Douglas, Basil Bernstein and Michael Halliday all drew attention to the significance of language in structuring and maintaining social life. During the eighties, this awareness of the social nature of language flooded into the mainstream of literacy education, having been given tremendous impetus by influences as diverse as the writings of Paolo Freire, the rise of poststructuralist theory (perhaps particularly in its feminist uses), the work of later social theorists such as Michel Foucault and Pierre Bourdieu, and the development of cultural studies as a favoured model in many tertiary English departments. By now we have had almost a decade of conceptualising literacy within this sociocultural framework, and the influence of this framing is in no danger of waning, as the various chapters in this book indicate.

In popular discourse, literacy is important because it provides an educated workforce who can further the economic goals of the nation. Literacy, it is believed (however erroneously, as discussed above), gets one a job. While still dominant in the minds of many politicians and indeed much of the general public, this concern with the utilitarian skills of basic reading and writing tends, in the discourse of English teaching at least during a great deal of the century, to have taken second place to the concern with literacy as an instrument of self-improvement. Whereas in earlier centuries the aim of teaching literacy had frequently been seen as aiding moral development through enabling people to read the Bible, from Matthew Arnold on, a similar moral work was considered to be being done by enabling people to read (or later write) creative texts.

The utilitarian and developmental traditions were often at swords drawn, but they had one thing in common: neither was working within a social theory that could illuminate what literacy teaching was doing as a social practice. With the explosion of social and cultural theory in the seventies and eighties, the way education, and particularly literacy teaching, worked to reproduce the dominant society became apparent and, to many, a matter of concern. Rather than just being concerned with literacy as a social phenomenon, literacy teaching gained a political edge. There came to be a real concern for using literacy teaching as a means to influence society, and particularly to overcome social inequity, whether by trying to ensure that all students had equal access to the kinds of literacy that mattered, or by exposing the workings of ideology in language.

Whereas language and literacy had previously been seen as being produced from an essential private self, the very existence of a self outside language and society was now being questioned. This stemmed from a much fuller theory of how language and texts operate to position people in a certain ideology and way of seeing the world. This led to the notion that, in fact, people might be constituted out of these ways of seeing the world, and so, in a very real sense, might be constructed within language. Our very identity, it appeared, might be made up of the language we used, the texts we produced and read.

If language was seen as central to making human beings what they are, it was also fundamental to the development of society and to keeping the society functioning smoothly, which, depending on one's political persuasions, might or might not be a good thing. The way in which power circulated in society through language became clearer. The complex ways in which social institutions depended on language, and the ways in which they shaped language to their particular purposes, became apparent.

Thus, while language could still certainly be seen as an instrument of empowerment that enabled people to operate productively in their social and personal lives, it could also be seen as the very thing that was constricting them into certain ways of thinking and being, and so seen as the shackles keeping them bound. Literacy teaching had suddenly become problematic. In terms of literacy 'skills', the work of teachers could be seen as fundamentally important in providing students with the means whereby they would have choices and could take their wished-for, valued and ideally remunerative place in the workforce and in society. On the other hand, it could simply be seen in the rather unflattering light of providing the next batch of fodder for offices and factories, with a few more able students being prepared for the heights of management, or at least of being the manager's secretary. In terms of inner self-development, teachers could be seen as giving students the means of independent thought and a richer understanding of the complexities of how their social world, indeed their very being, is constituted, but they could also be seen as simply reproducing in students the dominant ideologies of the society with the effect of making them docile and compliant cogs in the social machine.

Much of the theorising about literacy teaching in the last decade or so has been concerned to ensure that the positive outcomes are achieved and the negative ones avoided. Thus teachers often see themselves as trying to give all students access to the kinds of language and literacy that are the instruments of power, thereby enabling the less fortunate to overcome their disadvantage and achieve success. They also often see themselves as trying to expose the social limitations and the constrictions of thinking imposed by language, enabling the students to see how they are being positioned and limited, thereby hopefully enabling them to resist their enslavement.

Fundamental to both ways of working is the aim of making explicit how texts are working both in themselves and as instruments of social purposes. However, the very notion of a text has itself become problematic, and before we can look at some major current traditions of working with texts, we need to examine the question of what exactly a text might be.

Text and context

The term 'text' is used frequently in this book. Writers tend to use it in different ways, depending on their overall theoretical orientations, and there are in fact some differences among the contributors here. Together with its associated term 'context', the word 'text' has come into extensive use in literacy discussions in recent years.

The term 'text' actually comes from the Latin word for weaving: it refers to words and sentences woven together to create a single whole, one with 'texture'. We can see then that, even in its origins, the term is metaphorical. Just as a piece of cloth or a tapestry can be said to be woven together to create the finished piece, so too we can think of sets of language items working together to create the coherent thing we call a text. The word 'context' has an equally interesting and metaphorical history. It meant originally 'being woven together', where the prefix 'con' carried the sense of being together. Over the passage of the centuries it has come to refer to those elements that accompany a text, giving it meaning. The elements may be partly a feature of the physical setting in which language is used; but more importantly, they are also social and psychological, and part of the shared understandings that people need to have in order to create and/or comprehend a text and its purpose.

Putting together what all this suggests about text and context, we can see that any text is said to be comprehensible only in terms of the context which gives rise to it. Strictly, many linguists at least would say, context is known only because of the text which gives it life. Conversely, text is only known because of the context which makes it relevant.

Overall, we can say that a text is identifiable because it is meaningful: that is to say, it is a coherent passage of language in which some meaning is made. Texts may be of very variable lengths. Thus, a public notice saying 'Keep off the grass' is as much a text as a very long novel. The criterion for judging a text its always its coherence: does it 'hang together' in some way to build meaning?

While all that has been said so far relates to the notion of text as linguists use the term, it is important to note that today the term is used in many other related ways. This is of interest because it suggests that metaphor is again at work, as scholars and literacy theorists adopt the term to serve their purposes in the advancement of knowledge. Quite commonly today, for example, theorists write of visual images as texts. A visual text is said to differ from a verbal text, and this can be of interest for educational reasons. For example, it can open up questions to do with the relationship of the visual to the verbal text. How does the one complement the other? What kinds of meanings are made possible in the one that the other can't or doesn't construct? Williams, one of the contributors to this book, is interested in the manner in which young children prepare for the advent of reading behaviour. He considers early reading books in which there is no verbal text at all, yet their stories unfold entirely through the series of well-constructed images.

Misson, another contributor to this book, adopts poststructuralist perspectives upon the nature of text. He considers stories, examining the text of films as well as those of written narratives. For other theorists, not represented in this book, the notion of text is often used in other ways. For example, the human body is sometimes represented as a text, in which are inscribed various ideologies, attitudes and values giving the person identity. For others too, shopping malls or perhaps even individual buildings are theorised as texts, in which are realised ideologies of many kinds.

All these many ways of thinking about texts today arise from a related interest in another study: namely the study of semiotics. This is, literally, the study of the signs and symbols with which meanings are made. When we study meaning-making in humans, we study their semiosis: the various symbolic systems they use in order to construct their sense of the world, the multitude of relationships in which they engage, and the many forms of knowledge available to them. There are in fact many semiotic systems found in the contemporary world. Language itself is the principal semiotic system available to humans, but it always operates along with many other semiotic systems, such as music, dance, the visual arts, film, photography, dress and so on. All these semiotic systems can be said to involve the creation of texts in which significant meanings are made.

Frameworks for literacy teaching

The writers within this volume all work from a close consideration of the texts students read and write, just as they all subscribe to the notion that the most pertinent insights into literacy learning come from acknowledging its sociocultural framing. However, they are largely working within two different traditions. The one operates within a linguistic framework largely supplied by systemic functional (SF) linguistics developed by Halliday, Hasan, Martin and Matthiessen, to name a number of theorists. The other tradition works within a framework of poststructuralist cultural and social theory drawing on a range of theorists such as Foucault, Bourdieu, Althusser and Kristeva as filtered through the work of educationists such as Freire, Giroux and James Paul Gee. This latter tradition can be given the loose name of critical literacy. The two traditions are very far from opposed to each other, as can be seen in a number of the contributions to this volume. They can be linked together, and have been in the work of such writers as Fairclough, Kress and Lemke, and most significantly in Australia in the report of the team that made recommendations to government on strategies for the preservice preparation of teachers to teach English literacy (Christie *et al.*, 1991).

Systemic functional linguistics

The crucial aspect of SF linguistics for educational purposes lies in its functional nature. Rather than think of language as rules, as some traditions of language study have proposed, SF theory proposes that we think of language as offering systems of choices for making meaning. The choices we learn to make are functional in that they are relevant to building different kinds of meanings. The choices are not conscious (though some of them can be brought to consciousness in teaching-learning activities) and the choices are to do with the particular contexts of use in which people operate. Thus, for example, if one is in a job interview, the language choices one employs are rather different from those made, say, with family and friends over the dinner table, or perhaps with one's colleagues in a work situation. The language choices made in any context of use are said to be choices with respect to register. Just as a singer changes register from time to time, so too, metaphorically, a language user is said to change register depending upon the context.

The choices with respect to register are to do with the particular social activity *(field)*, the relationship between the participants in the interaction *(tenor)*, and the manner of communication *(mode)*. For example, the language differs depending on whether it is spoken or written, whether it is face to face, or distant, whether it accompanies pictorial information or not, and so on. In the late twentieth century the modes of language construction have become very various indeed. Language choices with respect to register are said to be made in terms of the ideational metafunction (i.e. choices that build the social activity and/or 'content' being constructed), the interpersonal metafunction (i.e. the choices that build the relationship), and the textual metafunction (i.e. the choices that organise the language into messages).

The educational relevance claimed for all this is that it is argued that when students in schools learn to use language they are learning to make relevant language choices for the construction of important kinds of meaning. The various school subjects or 'disciplines' represent ways of building information and ways of reasoning with that information. In order to understand the different kinds of information and their associated methods of reasoning, students must learn the language patterns in which these things are encoded. They must also learn the various text types or genres in which the knowledge is constructed.

A great deal of recent work in the SF tradition has been devoted to identifying the text types or genres students learn to read and write in order to be successful in their school learning. Genres are said to be structured in particular ways to achieve their purposes. In fact, a genre is said to be a 'staged, goal-oriented social process'. As it unfolds, its various stages all have a role in the organisation of information and experience. A procedural genre, of the kind found in a recipe book, for example, represents experience in a different set of stages, from say, an argumentative genre about the causes of pollution. Stories – and there are many kinds of stories – can also be shown to have particular sets of stages through which they unfold, entertaining and enlightening their readers or their listeners.

Genres can be said to be prototypical. They represent particular ways of organising and communicating meaning. Once people are familiar with them and competent in manipulating them, they can play around with them, often making subtle changes. Good writers in fact often play with the genre, but they do it, of course, against a background of the reader's expectations of the more standard pattern. Like other social phenomena, genres change over time, though perhaps written genres are more conservative than are spoken ones, so that they may change more slowly. Genres are not culture free, so whatever may be said of genres in English has no necessary relationship to what might be said of genres in other languages. Even within the international community of English speakers, different cultures will use the linguistic and textual resources available to them in somewhat different ways.

Genre theorists argue that it is because genres are so important for the building and communication of written information in particular, especially in educational settings, that they need to be the subject of overt teaching and learning. Some consciousness of the genre and its structure assists the student to become more competent in its uses. Such consciousness is also said to be an important step towards developing students able to critique a genre and the values and ideas it represents. It is in the latter sense that genre theory can connect with and, indeed, learn from, many of the perspectives drawn from critical literacy.

Critical literacy

Critical literacy is a pedagogy largely concerned with making explicit the ideological workings of texts. It is probably true that its analytical techniques are less specific and precise than those of the genre theorists, but it is probably also true that the theorisation of how ideology works through texts and how it creates the mind-set or subjectivity of the reader is more subtle and complex than that found in most genre theory. Indeed the subtlety and complexity of a great deal of the thought underlying critical literacy may well be something of a liability to it (just as the complexities of systemic functional grammar may prove inhibiting to those approaching work on texts within that tradition). Poststructuralist thought is not easy, particularly since much of it is counter-intuitive and asks us to be suspicious of the obvious and natural. Even more difficult is its refusal to take the self as a single, stable grounding for experiential knowledge. However, the insights into the nature of textuality and its close connections with how we are constituted as social beings provide a powerful agenda for classroom work.

Ideology, in much current thinking stemming largely from the work of Louis Althusser, works through representing the world to us in certain ways. Texts give us representations of the world that we acquiesce in because they correspond to our desires or because they show us our place in the larger scheme of things. It is thus we become the subject of ideology. We are the subject in two ways: the first in that we are subjected to the ideology of the representation, the second in that the ideology comes to constitute our subjectivity, our way of experiencing the world subjectively. We see an advertisement for coffee with an obviously well-off couple sitting down in their beautifully designed, warmly lit apartment, enjoying a quiet moment at the end of the day as they sip their coffee. Not only do we see this image as desirable, but we see ourselves as potentially inhabiting the image, being offered the image through the product. We consent to the kind of society and belief systems that aim at and produce these images of middle-class, consumerist, heterosexual contentment.

The main thrust of much work in critical literacy is towards analysing representations to make apparent the inherent ideology. Its aim is to render explicit the belief systems inscribed in the text and so negate their power. Since it is thought that ideology is at its most powerful when the representations through which it is being transmitted seem most natural, to denaturalise the naturalised image and show its constructedness and its tendentiousness is thought to defuse the ideology and make the student safe from its imposition. This does undoubtedly genuinely happen in some cases, but there must be some considerable doubt that the process is usually quite as simply effective as that. Ideology infiltrates our minds in particularly subtle and multifarious ways, and making explicit some of its workings does not necessarily free us from its multiplicitous grasp.

People are seen as being largely defined by their positioning in terms of class, ethnicity and gender. Much of the work in the classroom therefore is concerned to teach against limitations imposed on people in terms of one or other of these systems. This is done through analysis of the ideological implications of texts, examining how disadvantage is reproduced by constructing images that assume that certain qualities or ways of life are 'natural' to a certain group, or by looking at what is excluded from or not acknowledged in the way that a text is talking about a particular phenomenon. Excellent work has been done on teaching against discrimination, although it is worth noting that this, like anything else in the classroom, can become a rather empty routine. The students can produce the expected answer and mouth the appropriate sentiments without any notable impact on their actual attitudes.

The aim of critical literacy, in a phrase that stems from the work of Paolo Freire, is to enable students to 'read the word and the world' (Freire and Macedo, 1987). By doing this, they will come to a greater state of consciousness of how their lives are being limited by the society in which they are living, and there will thus be opened up for them the possibility of transforming, indeed liberating, both themselves and the society. The view thus baldly stated is undoubtedly both overly idealistic and rather simplistic in its conception of individual psychology and of how society works, but in its essential thrust it does provide a serious, attractive and challenging vision of what literacy teaching might achieve.

Information technology and literacy teaching

The area in which there is the greatest change in literacy practices at the moment is the area of information technology. Teachers and the general public have undoubtedly been continually rethinking literacy since writing was invented, but not since the advent of the printing press in the fifteenth century has there been anything with equal potential to revolutionise literacy as the advent of digital technology in all its different manifestations. The invention of a new medium for creating and disseminating verbal text has happened rarely in the history of humankind, and we are lucky enough to be witnessing it at the moment. Crucial questions about the nature and scope of literacy education are inevitably being opened up.

There are two aspects that are worth highlighting. The first is that the methods by which literacy is taught in classrooms are being changed by the use of the new learning technologies. This ranges from simple things like the use of presentation software packages in classrooms or computer programmes that aim to teach young children to read (see Morgan, this volume), through to the use of CD-ROM databases to research topics, or the use of the Internet to set up virtual classrooms across continents. The resources teachers and students have available to work with in literacy learning and teaching are being irrevocably changed as information and communication themselves are being transformed.

The second aspect signals an even more fundamental shift: literacy itself will inevitably change, indeed is already changing, has already changed. New literacy practices are developing and students will need to learn control of them. One of the most obvious examples of this is the use of e-mail. E-mail is often discussed as being a kind of writing that is almost a hybrid of writing and speech. This is only partly true since speech, like writing, can be formal or informal, but e-mail has certainly developed its own linguistic/stylistic conventions, and these are much more casual than is usual with writing. E-mail is perhaps most closely related to speech in that it is the kind of writing that can come closest to genuine dialogic interaction. If you send someone an e-mail message, they can reply immediately and then you can respond almost instantaneously to that. Moreover, you can break up their text and answer them point by point, and they can then do the same with your interventions, as the arrows on the side of the screen multiply to indicate the archaeological levels of the interaction. E-mail has developed its own protocols for appropriate exchanges, and its own typographical conventions, conventions that are often, when being explained, related to speech rather than writing (e.g. capitals are usually said to represent 'shouting' rather than 'emphasis').

Hypertext is another innovation of the digital revolution that will have a profound effect on our sense of what it is to read and write. While it is not true that we have always previously read text in a linear fashion from beginning to end – we have commonly used indexes to access different relevant bits of a larger text, jumped around from article to article in newspapers, read 'choose-your-own-adventure' books – it is certainly true that the multi-dimensional spatial lay-out of hypertext changes utterly the previously expected norm of linearity in over-all structure. We now have to get used to plunging ourselves into the unknown passages of the hypertextual world, where one hot-spot gateway after another can lead us into very strange and confusing places indeed. The usual metaphor of 'navigating' suggests the complexity and difficulty of working one's way through a hypertext. Not least of the difficulties sometimes, particularly with things such as hypertext narratives, is the fact that one does not know the full dimensions of the text, unlike a printed book: one navigates without map or orientation. This, of course, can be an immensely exciting feature of hypertext although some may see it as its frustration. Hypertext inevitably shatters our previous sense of textual structure. It forces us to think in multiple dimensions, with connections possible from any one point to any other. To analyse the genres being created and the particular ways in which the medium can be used to position us will take a great deal of research, and to teach the reading and writing of hypertext will take a great deal of rethinking literacy teaching based on that research.

One of the features of digital technology, of course, is that it is not just a verbal medium, but it makes the incorporation of graphic, tabular and even video material into composite texts very much easier. Hence the widespread use of the term 'multimedia' to cover a range of digital technology. We ought not forget in our excitement at the newness of all this that writing is itself a visual medium. If we allow that oral language is at least in some sense primary and written language a derivation, then the shift to written from oral language is a shift from the auditory to the visual channel. However, it is also true to say that, at least in these comparatively early days of digital technology, there is a sense in which one is more aware of the visual nature of digital text, presumably because a computer screen is what McLuhan calls a hot medium as opposed to the coolness and unobtrusiveness of the printed page. The digital text projects and asserts itself visually to us. The text is less stable in that the stroke of a key or the click of a button can delete or rearrange it, and that makes us more aware of the potential for design. While it is true that e-mail has developed an astonishing richness and ease of use in a mass of casual writing, it is also true that word processing, let alone desktop publishing, has made us more conscious than ever before of the visual design of the texts we produce. Again this is already having implications for the classroom and ways of teaching literacy.

To hark back to the theme of the social grounding of literacy, the new practices of literacy based on information technology exemplify the profound way in which culture is meshed with literacy practices. Information and communications technologies have transformed virtually every workplace, for example, and have often transformed the work relations within them; the Internet is developing new ways in which we relate to each other and to the rest of the world. These things have tremendous potential for positive transformation of our lives. However, the new literacy practices, like all literacy practices, can be used for the benefit of people or to their detriment. They can be used to extend people's social and intellectual horizons, or they can be used to limit their ways of thinking, as the common critique of lack of quality control on the Internet suggests. Literacy teachers still have the dual task of teaching students the understanding of literacy that will give them the greatest possibility of success in society, and of developing a critical awareness that will permit them to contest the uses of literacy aimed at constricting their thought. As always, creating a better life for students is one demand made on literacy, enabling them to evaluate critically the texts they meet is another.

The impulse behind this book has been to assert the breadth and richness of both literacy itself and literacy teaching. When literacy is raised as an issue in the media or parliament, the debate is usually framed within a narrow conception of literacy as a limited set of decoding skills within an equally narrow conception of its social purpose as somehow magically guaranteeing employment for the individual and success in international markets for the nation. The contributors to this volume, while arguing against neither the importance of basic reading skills nor the social importance of community literacy standards, are concerned to acknowledge the range and complexity of the issues involved in literacy as shown in the latest research, and to celebrate the achievement of literacy researchers and teachers. The different contributors therefore cover a wide range of themes, sites and practices concerned with literacy education.

We start with young children 'entering literate worlds'. Geoff Williams takes us on a tour through various aspects of early literacy learning. He looks first at the kind of literacy practices developed through picture books, including the capacities for decoding visual images that children are implicitly developing. He then shifts his attention explicitly to the classroom and demonstrates how young students can use a quite complex metalanguage in analysing the ways in which a text creates its meaning and its value system. The value for students in this is that it helps them develop a critical practice at the same time as it develops a complex awareness of how language works. It also gives them a metalanguage in which to talk about it.

Frances Christie in a sense takes up the story of the child progressing through school in her chapter, and looks at the development of student writing through the years of primary and secondary schooling. Through analysis of texts taken from different stages in schooling, she shows that literacy is not learnt once and for all in the early years, but new facets are constantly being learnt as students move on to the complex demands of the 'mature' genres of senior schooling. More than simply being learnt, she argues, an understanding of the linguistic demands must be explicitly taught. It is the responsibility of the teacher to develop an understanding of the writing requirements in the particular subject she/he is teaching, and to teach control of the linguistic features that mark out the kind of technical written language valued in particular subjects in schooling.

Not only do students need an understanding of how appropriate written forms are constructed so that they can reproduce them when required, but they also need such an understanding if they are to mount a satisfactory critique of texts in those forms. This is a major theme in the chapter by Mary Macken-Horarik. Building on a concern with the contextualisation of all reading and writing, Macken-Horarik develops the notion of intertextuality as a key concept for understanding the ways in which texts are constructed for particular purposes, and for mounting a critique of what those texts are doing. In several examples taken from classroom practice she shows how teachers have created lesson sequences that progress from teaching about the writing demands of a particular subject and topic to developing a critical awareness of the texts involved.

Students read both in and out of school, although the material they read and the reading practices vary enormously between the two sites. Students do read print texts out of school, but much of the 'reading' students do in their spare time is of non-print texts. It is also true that when reading a text for purposes of entertainment, a different kind of engagement occurs from that involved in reading texts for school purposes. Ray Misson looks at some of the ways in which fictional texts, both print and non-print, involve and position their readers, and argues that an awareness of these textual strategies needs to be taught to students to develop their critical capacities.

As noted above, information technology has created new kinds of texts and this inevitably has immense implications for literacy teaching. Wendy Morgan takes us to a number of classrooms in which information technology is being used for a variety of purposes. She not only gives us a rich sense of the possibilities being opened up for teachers and students by digital technology, but, working within a critical framework that theorises in sociocultural terms the literacy practices she discovers in the classrooms, she institutes a serious discussion of the benefits and limitations of such activities.

In a wide-ranging final chapter, Colin Lankshear and Michele Knobel look at what it means to read and write, before examining some of the conceptions of literacy underlying reading programmes in the light of this more complex conception. Then, by examining a number of case studies of individual students using computer technology, they remind us of the rich literacy practices students can engage in out of school, practices that have clear and immediate social purposes. These practices are scarcely reflected in the kind of work being done in school at all. The implications for schools, if they wish to be relevant to the students' and society's needs, are clear.

Since literacy is so bound up with society, literacy is always changing because society is always changing. Teachers have to continually rethink what they do if their practice is not to become irrelevant or moribund. The contributors to this book, working from a base in educational research, all give a sense of ways in which renewal can and is happening. They give, we hope, a rich sense of the possibilities and the challenges facing all literacy educators.

Reference

Christie, F. *et al.* (1991) *Teaching English Literacy: A Project of National Significance on the Preservice Preparation of Teachers for Teaching English Literacy*, Darwin: Centre for Studies of Language in Education.

Freire, P. and Macedo, D. (1987) *Literacy: Reading the Word and the World*, Massachusetts, Bergin and Garvey.

2

Children entering literate worlds

Perspectives from the study of textual practices

Geoff Williams

Introduction

Public concern about children's development of competence to read and write is an important social fact, but media and political responses to this concern are often very simple. Media reports, and the political policies in which they frequently result, often suggest that useful directions for literacy education policy are to be found in imaginary visions of learning and teaching which are located in the halcyon days of nobody's youth. As a result, public discussion of what is involved in learning to be literate as a child in the late twentieth century is often reduced to considering reincarnations of ideas which are more typical of the late nineteenth.

The processes through which young children enter the various literate worlds of experience in our age are complex. As a consequence, people who are seriously interested in young children's literacy education require robust theory and methods of description to assist their efforts on behalf of children. The problem is: where should one begin to look for usefully robust theory since there is no shortage of advocates in a confusing range of alternatives? My own approach is to begin from a rather straightforward observation: that people read and write chiefly in order to make meaning in the living of their lives. Since in making meaning people produce texts, and they typically do so by interacting socially with other people, these texts are part of what might generally be called 'textual practices' in the culture. So I look for useful theory in all of those disciplines which are interested in exploring literacy as an aspect of textual practices.

In this chapter I propose to take up three features of advances in the study of textual practices in order to illustrate how they might inform literacy education policy and practice. They are illustrations only, selected from a wide range of issues which can be illuminated from this perspective. They are chosen largely for their relevance to challenging much of the taken-for-granted in public discourse about early literacy development.

The first feature is the question of young children's learning through picture books, especially those which involve subtle relations between visual and linguistic meanings. Of course, picture books are often thought to be important adjuncts to early literacy 'programmes' since they entertain and motivate children, and sometimes they are thought to have a more central place in classroom literacy work, as the major textual basis for children's entry to literacy because of qualities of language and visual image. Rarely, though, have their specific qualities as texts which are patterned simultaneously through two sets of meaning modalities been considered, and it is this feature I will take up. The key question here is: what possibilities for children's literacy learning are created by various relations between language and image in children's picture books, beyond the obvious advantages of entertainment and reading pleasure?

The second feature is a rather vexed question in English-speaking systems of education, that of the use and misuse of 'grammar' teaching in young children's education. Pressure to reintroduce or extend the study of grammar in school curricula is an obvious phenomenon of the last decade across most English-speaking countries. The discourse revolves around an attempt to return to disciplinary practices of the 1950s and 1960s, rather than any real enthusiasm for advancing children's knowledge about language and certainly not the prospect of enabling them to be critical of textual practices. Such pressure has resulted, understandably enough, in a resistance to grammatical study amongst primary teachers or at best a minimalist approach which results in children encountering grammar typically as descriptions of classes of words. A too-frequent expression of the recurrence of grammar teaching has been questions such as: 'underline the nouns in this sentence'. To which children might (and do) reasonably reply: 'why?' Sometimes isolated facts such as 'there has to be agreement of number between subject and verb', introduced to children as 'language rules' determining correct practice, substitute for substantive views of how language is structured to encode meaning. Teachers quite understandably fear that this expansion will be at the expense of some other hard-won gains which have made entry into school literacy more meaningful and positive for a large number of children. However, I shall argue that awareness of grammatical structure and use of it in practical literacy tasks can have a positive, significant place in early literacy development. The key point is a linguistic one. What kind of grammar is an appropriate grammar for teaching and learning in the early years of schooling? I argue against the reintroduction of traditional school grammar, but for some specific uses of grammatical knowledge under specific practical conditions. (Arguing against traditional school grammar does not entail the view that a knowledge of elementary grammatical classes is irrelevant.) To develop the discussion I shall draw on examples of classroom work with young children, which are part of an ongoing research project based at the University of Sydney.

The third feature is the complex problem of variation in literate practices in different social locations. Recent work in linguistics on this problem seems to offer some of the best opportunities for understanding the wide range of children's success in school literacy, and for doing something specific about narrowing that range in a positive direction. The extent of the range is evident from very early in children's school experience, as we know from surveys of literacy development during the first two or three years of formal schooling (Wells, 1985). For that reason alone it is worth inquiring carefully about different varieties of literate practices in families in different social locations, and their various complex links with school literacy practices. If there is variation then it is obvious that not all variants can logically stand in equal relation to school practices. Which variants, correlated with which social locations, are most closely linked to school practices and what are the likely effects for children entering the literate world of kindergarten classrooms?

Before I begin to discuss these issues in more detail it may be useful to say something further about the sense of 'textual practices' used here, since this idea is not typically a key concept in dominant forms of literacy education.

Textual practices

By textual practices I mean those occasions in which people use various resources which the culture makes available to them *to mean* as they live life in real social contexts. From this perspective, texts are the outcome of engaging in social activities of various kinds. To make meaning in social life we typically use a range of different modalities – for example, gesture, visual image and, of course, language. Of these modalities it is language which is the most extensively used. It is also, distinctively, the modality which enables us to reflect back on textual practices most readily, making them an object of study as well as an expression of other social activities.

It follows that analyses of the language used in social life may yield useful insights into social processes, including for our present purposes, processes of human development. In the case of very young children much meaning is of course initially carried by gesture, with small patterns of sound gradually coming systematically to signify features of a child's individual meanings until the child, with the benefit of months of being treated as a real meaning-maker, begins to use the semantics and grammar of the first language reciprocally with family members. Looking from a quite different developmental perspective, this time the evolution of legal texts in the culture over the last two thousand years, we notice that legal texts rely on structures of writing which are to be read in highly regulated ways within complex institutional practices. Human development of the ability to manage the latter, having begun with the former about twenty years or so earlier, is deserving of both respect and careful research attention.

In thinking about early literacy development in terms of textual practices we are able to take account of some effects of multi-modal texts, in this case texts which mean through language and visual image. Meaning is created both within language and image and, very importantly, *between* language and image. Lewis Carroll has Alice ask, appropriately enough, 'What is the use of a book without pictures or conversation?' Pictures, as Alice knew well, entertain and delight. Do they also instruct in ways important for subsequent development?

Focussing on textual practices is also a way to consider children's use of language in reflection on meaning-making. That is to say, the texts children speak, write and read are not just expressions of engagement with immediate experiences. Frequently, these texts are also linguistic reflections on that experience. They are examples of language turning back on itself to understand more about the terms of its making, and they provide a very useful perspective from which to consider any potential for children to use grammatical description. It is a perspective qualitatively different from that given by the media in linking grammatical study with authoritarian ideas about standards of language use.

For example, we know from Chukovsky (1968) and many other scholars that at a young age children use language as a resource for thinking about language itself. Chukovsky observed how children played with typical relations in a field of knowledge by inverting them:

Frogs fly in the sky,
Fish sit in fisherman's laps.
Mice catch cats
And lock them up in
Mousetraps.

Children's huge interest in jokes is further evidence. For example, a young friend, Ben, used often to ask me the following riddle:

Question: What is orange all over and sounds like a parrot? Answer: A carrot.

Obviously one factor in Ben's enjoyment was the surprise the riddle creates, and the response he received from his audiences as a consequence. But what of the language itself? The language of children's jokes about language is particularly worth considering for what it reveals about children's interest in reflecting on language.

Considering language play from a linguistic perspective we are able to see that play explores language across all of its strata, from differences between phonemes and effects of their patterning in words and texts through grammar to generic structures. Ben's joke, for example, relies primarily on a turn of grammar ('sounds' as a process of material action versus 'sounds' as a process of comparative relationship). (See Christie's chapter in this volume for some discussion of grammatical processes.) On phonemic distinctions and patterns, we have children's enthusiasm for Dr

Seuss across generations. On play with generic structure, here is an example of a children's schoolyard joke noted by June Factor:

What is red and round and goes at 120 m.p.h.?
A tomato. I lied about the speed.

The generic conventions are violated, and we are cheated!

If linguistic play is a prominent aspect of textual practice in children's lives, and proto-investigations of grammar form part of that play, is it possible for this 'natural' feature of childhood to be extended by introducing to children conceptual tools which enable them to enhance the range and depth of play? After all, we do just that in early childhood with structured equipment of various kinds. And in mathematics we do so from the first years of schooling, with tools to enable children to reflect on structures of number and space. Is it possible to do so with language? It is this question which is the focus of the discussion of grammar learning and literacy development in primary education which forms the focus of the second part of this chapter.

In the third part of this chapter the focus will be variation in discussion of written language in families, and relationships of variants to school practice. Again, the sense of textual practice is useful because it directs attention to what people actually *do* in talking about written text with young children, in the sense of what kinds of meanings they are typically interested in and produce in different types of context, not what they *can* do in dislocated instances of language production. The orientation to textual practice draws attention to the habitual ways in which people may talk about written texts to young children, and some of the consequences of these for early literacy learning in school.

Image–language relations in literacy development

Textual practices, then, are the base for this discussion. However, if we examine research on early literacy development it soon becomes obvious that text, as situated acts of linguistic meaning, plays no part in typical research perspectives. One authority on children's literacy development, speaking from a lifetime working on questions of children's reading success and difficulty, comments:

In all of the books I have read about reading and teaching reading there is scarcely a mention about what is to be read. Books are, as the saying goes, taken as read in the discussions about reading teaching. The reading experts, for all their understanding about 'the reading process', treat all text as the neutral substance on which the process works, as if the reader did the same thing with a poem, a timetable, a warning notice.

(Meek, 1988: 5)

Or, we might add, the same thing with a reading scheme booklet and a picture book. Or with a well-written factual text and a picture book.

The reason for this major gap in our knowledge is that most research has focussed attention on individual features of children. If we were to construct a diagram of the typical orientation to research, reduced to the most simple elements to enable contrast, it would look like figure 2.1. Here the process of reading is understood in terms of various 'mental' processes to do with perception, such as those of recognition, memory and attention. Obviously these *are* very important processes in children's development. In fact it could be argued, following Vygotsky, that mediated processes of voluntary attention are basic to the development of abstract thought, and are importantly variable (Vygotsky, 1981). But the problem with isolating these processes in the way the model suggests is this: how are we to understand the processes adequately in the absence of an account of what children are attending to? It is simply not the case that the texts a young child reads, or is read, are a neutral substance, without any agency in developing reading competences. Such a view would be directly analogous to arguing that the nature of the conversations a child hears and participates in from birth are inconsequential to the development of oral language. Any parent will tell us that is false, and of course a large number of research studies confirm this view (for example, Halliday, 1975; Fox, 1993; Hasan, 1989, 1991, 1992; Heath, 1983; Painter, 1996).

An alternative approach is to orient enquiries with an image such as in figure 2.2. The emphasis is markedly changed. Here text is regarded as *agentive* in forming the nature of the process in which a child can engage, though children are also afforded an equally active role. They are engaging in complex processes of interpretation which are made possible by the nature of the texts they read and discuss. It is what I understand to be implied by the term 'interactive reading development'. Later, this model will require extension in order to refine what is meant by the apparently obvious terms 'children' and 'text', but it can be used as a temporary basis to explore textual roles in reading development more specifically.

To do so the discussion has obviously to focus on some specific texts, and questions about specific competences. One such question is: how do you learn about the episodic nature of written narrative, and relations

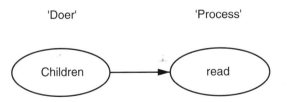

Figure 2.1 An initial model of reading as 'decontextualised' process

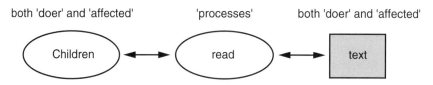

both 'doer' and 'affected'   'processes'   both 'doer' and 'affected'

Figure 2.2 A partial model of reading as 'interactive' process

between episodes and endings? It is a complex question but it is also a practical one since some children do seem to experience difficulty in under-standing relations between specific textual elements and meanings of the whole, depending on their experience with varieties of written text when they enter school. Notice that different views about language will deter-mine views both about how significant the question is, and what language features are important in narrative text.

Children's variable understanding of relations between episodes and endings was actually a practical issue I had to ask myself recently when researching the literacy learning difficulties experienced by some six-year-old children in inner-city Sydney schools. They were bright, excited children, but very frustrated by school literacy demands and generally unsuccessful in meeting their schools' expectations. It soon became clear, through looking systematically at the language of the texts which these 'low-achievers' were reading, that the texts themselves were impeding children's learning and in fact creating many of the difficulties we observed. In attempting to make reading material simple the writers of the reading scheme had constructed small recounts of discrete events, with each double page spread presenting a separate recount. (The events were not really recognisable as stories.) For example, in one text each separate recount concerned an episode about a helicopter, but there was no relationship between the separate events. The texts were incoherent, formally speaking.

It is possible, of course, to write a simple, accessible text which is coherent, in the sense that each of the episodes relates to the others and builds towards some significant moment – a climax, perhaps. *I Went Walking* (Machin and Vivas, 1989) is an example. The first impression of this book is its striking simplicity – large illustrations with a lot of white space, a maximum of two lines of print on a page, extensive repetition in the language. It relates a simple story of a child's walk, discovery of various animals who are partly disguised, then a carnivalesque ending in which the child protagonist and the animals celebrate enthusiastically. The text is structured by a series of simple episodes: discovery of a black cat, a horse, a cow, a duck, and so on, all of which follow the child secretly to the celebration.

The language is also highly patterned, which is to say something different from the fact that it is repetitive. Many of the same words do recur but the repetition is functional in building meaning in a way quite different from 'the helicopters' text. A pattern is built up, then the pattern is broken at the climax to foreground the significance of a particular, celebratory event. If we shift focus for a moment to theorists of literature we can see that this is precisely a textual strategy argued to be distinctive about literary texts – the foregrounding of language features because they stand out against text-internal norms (Hasan, 1985; Mukarovsky, 1977). So in *I Went Walking* we not only have a basic coherence which is crucial for the text as a unit of meaning, but we have a particular type of coherence in the patterning of language, which in a simple way is an instance of significant reading and writing practices in Western culture (see figure 2.3). The text is, then, not just an enjoyable venue through which to encourage children's reading nor a venue to practise decoding, but an agent in developing understanding of how texts in this range of registers mean.

The images are also, as one would expect, highly patterned. On the first double page spread a clear reading path is established from the child, following his or her glance, across the logs in the basket and on through the next spread until the path stops at the enclosed, circular form of the child and the cat together. The pause in the flow of the images co-occurs with the end of the linguistically construed episode. Similarly, there is a clear reading path from the left of the next page, tracking a few strands of a tail and then on and around the solid body of the horse to pause. And so on for each episode. These are simple but not inconsequential matters, I think, in assessing the contribution of text to the development of reading competence.

Here is a rather more complex question on the same general theme: how does one first learn to take up a point of view in reading fictive narrative? That is, how does one begin to learn to act like the 'model reader' of a text, to deploy the term that the Italian semiotician, Umberto Eco, has recently reintroduced in his Norton Lectures (Eco, 1995)? Eco describes a 'model' reader as 'a sort of ideal type whom the text not only foresees as a collaborator but also tries to create' (1995: 9). The idea might be expressed in a parallel way as the linguistically constructed addressee of a text, the sort of 'reader' who understands the consequences of 'and it was still hot' at the end of *Where the Wild Things Are*.[1]

Perhaps an even more important question about point of view for the early development of reading is this: how does one learn to shift point of view in response to new information, as subtle nuances of voice become available through the design of a text? Evidently this has to be achieved through experience of text, since it is a matter of learning the appropriate tenor of relationship with a narrator of fiction. Is the narrator straightforward in giving me information, or is he/she unreliable so that I have to read beyond the congruent meanings to infer a different orientation?

How could texts offer experiences of different points of view and different qualities of narration to the relatively inexperienced?

What did you see?

I went walking.

I saw a black cat
Looking at me.

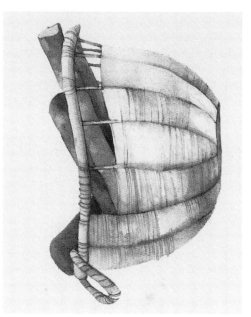

Figure 2.3 Excerpt from *I Went Walking* (Machin and Vivas, 1989)

Anthony Browne's *Gorilla* (Browne, 1983) is an interesting text to consider since even at a first glance the images evidently involve different points of view. I will use it as the basis for the following discussion, together with some examples from Sendak's *Where the Wild Things Are* (Sendak, 1967) and Baillie and Tanner's *Drac and the Gremlin* (Baillie and Tanner, 1988).

A common element one notices in many picture books is that a point of departure is unambiguously established, typically through an image of the focalising character in the first major illustration. In *Gorilla* we first see the protagonist Hannah absorbed in solitary reading about gorillas, her passion evident in her line drawing pinned to the wallpaper. The opening image of *Where the Wild Things Are* is similar: a mischievous Max hammering nails into a wall. In *Drac and the Gremlin* the first image is the face of the protagonist Drac, open and smiling, as if inviting readers into the fantastic game in her garden, which begins to unfold on the next page. So one ready answer to the first question is that picture books often offer a striking image of the character whose point of view is to orient the narrative.

This simple sense of orientation has, however, to be extended to take account of more subtlety. In *Gorilla* the initial image does not simply present Hannah as focalising character: it also suggests how a reader might think about Hannah through positioning the viewer *in relation to* the character. In order to refine the analysis some 'meta' resources have to be brought into play here, resources which enable different facets of meaning to be studied both in this specific instance and across a range of images. What one essentially needs is a way of talking about the details of meaning making in visual images which nets in not only representational features such as who is doing what to whom, but also features of interaction between viewers and represented figures. For this purpose I will use some proposals for semiotic work by Kress and van Leeuwen in their recent *Reading Images* (1996). As Kress and van Leeuwen point out, grammars of visual images are in their infancy when compared to grammars of language, where centuries of work have led to the range of sophisticated descriptions now available. It is therefore to be expected that descriptive resources will require some extension as they are used across a range of contexts (see, for example, the refinement of their approach by Kress and van Leeuwen themselves (1990, 1996)). Nevertheless, the resources do markedly enhance an understanding of how visual images mean.

In the first image of *Gorilla*, how is a reader positioned in relation to Hannah? One interesting feature is the high angle of viewing: the reader 'looks down' on Hannah from a higher position. This angle is more or less repeated in the second image, a kitchen scene in which Hannah and her father are engaged in solitary activity. Looking through the text one sees that the vertical angle of viewing varies considerably, and in quite a systematic way in relation to the plot. Contrast the first two images with that in which the gorilla 'looks down' on both the viewer and Hannah in bed. Further, the vertical angle in the first kitchen scene is quite different from that in the second kitchen scene, which is the penultimate image in the text. There the viewer is at eye level with Hannah and her father. Does this variation achieve any significance? Kress and van Leeuwen suggest that it does, that it is not simply an arbitrary feature or the result of an illustrator's whim. On their description a high angle encodes a sense of the greater power of the reader/viewer whereas a low angle creates a sense of the greater power of the figure in the image, the represented participant. Using this description we might 'read' Hannah in the first and second image as 'just a little child'. However, a significant change comes in the fourth image, in which Hannah makes a request to her father. He is depicted writing at a desk, his back to her, while she looks up to him. Here the reader takes up a vertical angle which is an exaggeration of Hannah's perspective; exaggerated by virtue of the lower vertical angle, but from a parallel horizontal position. The reader is no longer positioned as just an observer of the girl, but literally associated with her perspective by taking on a similar power position in relation to the father.

We can test the idea further by looking at vertical angle in *Where the Wild Things Are*. Here we see that in the first images viewers are positioned in a vertical angle from which they look down on the mischievous Max. However, there is a major change at a strategic point in the plot, where Max 'sailed off through night and day'. Here the viewing angle drops quite dramatically so that now the reader looks up into Max's smiling, conspiratorial face. He has become the leader in quite a different dance.

There is, again, considerable variation through the text, variation which is clearly associated with plot development. For example, the angles vary in the three central images as Max's power increases: from co-dancer, where there is a ninety degree angle of viewing, to king of all wild things, where there is a steep low angle. By the final image, where Max is restored to his bedroom, the angle is again high, suggesting Max is now restored to his 'normal' state of power. The general significance of the vertical angle becomes obvious if we contemplate the likely effect on child readers if the text were to finish with an image of Max, or even more so an image of one of the wild things, from a low vertical angle.

These observations enable ways of talking about the construal of point of view in picture books to be extended considerably. It becomes possible to move from the simple identification of the focalising character, the character who is the point of departure in a reading of the narrative, to the interpersonal relation with the character which a reader might make. What is particularly interesting about *Gorilla* is that there is no stable relation with respect to power between the reader and the focalising character. Sometimes the reader's perspective parallels that of Hannah, as in viewing the orang-utan and chimpanzee. That is, the reader's point of view is linked directly to that of the character. At other times the relationship is more distant, with the viewer observing Hannah from a low vertical angle, as when Hannah first picks up the toy gorilla. As a result of the variation a child reader cannot just associate with Hannah's orientation, at least in the simple sense of identification. Rather, and this point is very important for discussion of entry into literate practices, readers are *simultaneously* positioned as both part of the emotion of the narrativised experience and somewhat detached from it as observer of Hannah's actions and responses.

Looking again at the second image in the text, that of Hannah at the breakfast table with her father, a reader is likely to be struck by the distinctiveness of the shapes and colours of this kitchen. They are very desaturated colours, flattened three-dimensional objects and regular geometric shapes. It is a cold, abstracted, perhaps rather clinical environment. It is certainly in sharp contrast with the later image in which Hannah and her father are together, where there is a high degree of colour saturation, irregular shapes and a greater depth of field. Kress and van Leeuwen argue that these features affect our sense of the 'reality' of the constructed world. Their analysis suggests that the abstracted features of *Gorilla* are associated with a sense of low modality, a relatively uncertain, problematic world: a statement such as 'this is how the world might be' rather than 'this is how the world is'. In contrast, the high colour saturation and greater depth of field in the later image gives sense of a much higher modality, a more certain world.

However, if we go back again to the second image it is clear that things are not quite so simple. Not all of the elements are desaturated and abstracted. Hannah herself is represented in rich colour, with the detail of her hair very clear and the chair she is sitting on is also represented in detail – the grain of the wood, for example, is visible. So there is some difference, and therefore some complexity. What is the significance of the variation?

My reading is influenced by the fact that the viewer's horizontal positioning here parallels Hannah's. The reader may construct a sense of Hannah's situation by looking from her perspective, but with the important condition that the experience is not very certain. The room and the father seem cold, distant and boring, but we cannot be as certain that this is actually so as we can be certain that Hannah is 'seeing' this element of her world in this way. So when the narrator tells a reader 'Her father didn't have time to take her to see one at the zoo. He didn't have time for anything', there is the problem of the 'truth status' of the comment and the tone of voice through which to read it. Is this the case, or is it what Hannah feels to be the case? Nothing in the language directly signals irony. It has, rather, to be inferred from the context and the internal variation in the image. Experienced readers will almost certainly read the language as ironic because they know the situation so well. It is the kind in which a young child explodes, 'Oh! You never do anything that I want to do!' But a child's reading position is not the same, and the potential for irony has to be learnt through the resources a text makes available, and obviously discourse around that text. How, in turn, that discourse might be both structured and structuring of consciousness about textuality would take us a long way beyond our focus, but it is one of the least examined and more fascinating questions yet to be considered in detail in the early literacy field.

For an experienced reader the tone of narratorial voice will perhaps be reminiscent of the tone of the narratorial comment in *Sense and Sensibility* (Austen 1961):

> This argument was irresistible. It gave to his intentions whatever of decision was wanting before; and he finally resolved, that it would be absolutely necessary, if not highly indecorous, to do more for the widow and children of his father, than such kind of neighbourly acts as his own wife pointed out.

My copy of *Sense and Sensibility* quotes a jingle Jane Austen is reputed to have written:

> I do not write for such dull elves
> As have not a great deal of ingenuity themselves.

How does a child come to 'have' that kind of ingenuity in reading fictive narrative? It is difficult to imagine how interpretive ingenuity could be developed without access to texts which create the subtle play of relevant semantic qualities. This is not, though, the accepted view currently informing early literacy pedagogy.

One potential of detailed linguistic and semiotic work on picture book texts is to provide a basis for rethinking the kinds of activity around a text which young children are required to complete. There is a terrible banality in much of what constitutes the 'activity' phase of lessons in early school literacy, unrelated to developing understanding of either what or how texts mean (Christie, 1990). To say so is not, of course, to make a criticism of teachers as individual professionals, but rather of a particular type of pedagogic discourse, derived indirectly and often inaccurately from theories of children's limited abilities to think abstractly during the primary years. It is particularly the *how* of meaning which has been marginalised in pedagogic discourse, yet what could be more apposite to understanding the range of literate worlds which children must enter in order to be members of a contemporary culture? Much of the problem revolves, I think, around views of language, particularly language with which to describe language, and it is to this issue I now move.

Young children, grammar and literacy development

Given the rather fraught political context for this discussion, it must necessarily begin from an assertion that achievements by teachers in the early literacy field to make literacy work in schools more active, more meaningful and more pleasurable must be held constant. Children's pleasure in reading must be the first priority. Their delight, their laughter, sometimes their profound silence at the end of a reading of a text, must be retained. As well, their freedom to range across texts of different kinds, texts by R. L. Stine, John Burningham, Phillipa Pearce, Maurice Sendak, Paul Jennings, Anthony Browne, Nadia Wheatley, Aidan Chambers and Enid Blyton. And their sense of freedom to experiment, to write and read spontaneously as a matter of personal interest and choice. Having this basis secure, is it then possible to build on young children's interest in language as an object of reflection by introducing to them tools which enable them to describe language, the better to understand how it works?

It may very well be possible, provided that the grammatical tools allow children to describe structure from the perspective of meaning, which is to say that the grammar has to be a functional one. Not all grammars describe structure in the same way. Very evidently, traditional school grammars have not been much concerned with meaning. To confirm this one has only to look at examination papers in English in the early 1960s. Carter provides a graphic illustration from a GCE paper:

> Leaving childhood behind, I soon lost this desire to possess a goldfish. It is difficult to persuade oneself that a goldfish is happy and as soon as we have begun to doubt that some poor creature enjoys living with us we can take no pleasure in its company.
>
> Using a new line for each, select *one* example from the above passage of *each* of the following:

(i)   an infinitive used as the direct object of the verb;
(ii) an infinitive used in apposition to a pronoun;
(iii) a gerund;
(iv) a present participle

(Carter, 1996:1–2)

There is obviously nothing about meaning here, but merely and miserably a focus on a kind of grammatical knowledge for its own sake. Children themselves are rightly scathing in criticism of this kind of teaching. In research I have been conducting we have asked children their views about the traditional grammar they had learned previously in school. Here, for instance, is what Tim said during a discussion with a research associate, Joan Rothery:

Joan: Would you like to learn more of that kind of grammar [i.e. traditional school grammar]?
Tim: Well the thing is you think you've learned it all, pronouns, verbs.
Joan: Well how did you learn things like pronouns, verbs etc.?

Tim: Well that was just normal classwork we used to do.

Joan: In another class?

Tim: Yes. You've got fifteen words, now you've got a box, in this box there are nouns and in this box there are adjectives [*inaudible*]

Joan: Right.

Tim: What's this got to do with anything? The teacher would just say 'It's grown up teaching'.

Children require that they understand the purpose of their abstract study of language. 'It will be useful later' is not a satisfactory basis in the absence of a strong, broader sense of purpose. However, for a long time observations of children's entirely understandable frustration in learning traditional school grammar have served as evidence for the conclusion that they are uninterested in reflecting on language. This reasoning is deeply flawed. One way to test the claim is, obviously, to ask children what they think language is, and what questions they might have about it.

When we did so as part of the project to which I have just referred, we were taken aback at how much children had to say, and by how much technical knowledge they had gained. We asked children to talk in small groups about the question 'What is language?', then to construct a diagram of their understandings. One group of eleven-year-olds built up on a classroom wall a large 'mind map' of various elements of language they knew about, and questions they had. Hans was an expert on dialect, for example, since his country of birth was Austria and his first language German. His account of the variation in German spoken in different countries greatly intrigued the children. Tamilselvan taught children about the Tamil alphabet, and Kate showed them how to write a range of ideographs. Their questions about language were intriguing: how many dialects are spoken in Asia; what is the world's largest dictionary; what do linguists actually do when they study language, and so on. Their observations about grammar at this first stage of discussion were particularly interesting. Their view was that grammar was straightforwardly about language rules, about correct usage in writing. They were much less certain about relations between grammar and speech!

Children are very interested in knowing more about language, judged by the evidence of their spontaneous play *with* language, their exploratory play *about* language and their more abstract, systematic reflections *on* it. The issue in language curriculum is not so much children and their capacities to reflect on language but rather the tools for reflection which are available to them. It may well be that different means to describe language structure, means which children can perceive to be useful in their immediate contexts, would enable qualitatively different levels of understanding to be achieved.

In the research to which I have been referring earlier we have been studying the first moments of six-year-old children's understanding of a functional grammar. The children were in Year 1 in the New South Wales school system, in a school located in the inner suburban region. About 65 per cent spoke a language other than English as mother tongue. Their teacher described herself as lacking any systematic knowledge about grammar, having not been introduced to grammatical description at school or during her teacher education. This lack of opportunity made her the more interested to learn about language structure alongside the children.

Such a study of course requires that a large range of evidence be gathered from different perspectives: data such as detailed classroom observation and videotaping as well as transcripts of small-group and whole-class discussion, children's written work samples, individual conversations between researchers and children about their learning, their work with grammatical puzzles and so on. Obviously only a tiny fragment can be introduced here. Since so little is heard from children in discussions about grammar learning I will illustrate some of the first moments of attending to structure through some excerpts from transcripts of classroom discourse.

A book the children were reading at this time with great enjoyment was *Piggybook* (Browne, 1986). The first few sentences give a good sense of the book's thematic concern.

> Mr Piggott lived with his two sons, Simon and Patrick, in a nice house with a nice garden, and a nice car in the nice garage. Inside the house was his wife. 'Hurry up with the breakfast, dear,' he called every morning, before he went off to his very important job. 'Hurry up with the breakfast, Mum,' Simon and Patrick called before they went off to their very important school.

The text makes an ironic comment on gender and domestic work by portraying the males first as lazy chauvinists then, after the overburdened mother leaves the family temporarily, as grossly incompetent housekeepers and finally as happy to share the domestic work. The mother has time under the new arrangements to mend the car!

One of the features to which the children were particularly attracted was the progressive transformation of the house into a pigsty after the mother had gone away. As well as the metaphoric sense of pigsty, the grossness of the unwashed dishes and filthy floors, there was a somewhat more literal sense too as light switches transformed to pigs' faces, wallpaper decoration changed from fleur-de-lys to pigs' feet and the males themselves assumed the shape of pigs. The children enthusiastically searched for details of visual patterns and this became a ready basis for a search for linguistic patterns. The key, of course, was to provide some resource which would help them to see the patterning of language as readily as they could see the visual patterning. No small task.

Here I will concentrate on the first moments of attention to verbs of speech, verbs such as 'say' or 'yell'. These verbs we called 'saying processes', following the descriptive principles of systemic functional grammar, where they are called verbal processes (Halliday, 1994; Matthiessen, 1996). The teacher introduced the discussion of grammar by focussing on dialogue (recall Alice's interest in books with pictures and conversation).

Teacher	So when you have people talking in books you find these talking marks and speaking marks around the words that they're saying. And what is usually after those? For example, if I asked . . . What would be something Miss Patricia [*the teacher*] would say? Denise?
Denise	'Sit down children.'
Teacher	Alright. 'Sit down children'. What would go after that? Angelica?
Angelica	Said Miss Patricia.
Teacher	Said Miss Patricia. Very good. So 'said' is a saying process. What about if I had 'Help me!'? What could go after that?. . . 'Help me!'
Child	[*inaudible*]
Sean	Said Tony.

The children's orientation to description here is contextual rather than immediately structural. They use the context, in the senses both of their familiarity with this text and their prior knowledge of the patterning of speech in written language, to make a first step into discriminating an element of the grammatical structure. The teacher then extends this first sense of the function of the grammatical element by drawing attention to the uses of variation.

Teacher:	Alright. So, you could, I could say, 'Help me, Miss Patricia'. What if, about if I said 'Help me!' [*shouting*] Pachana?
Pachana:	Loud.
Teacher:	*Or could I say 'Help me' [*more quietly; asterisks signify simultaneous speech*]
Pachana:	*Yelled Miss Patricia.
Teacher:	What did you say?
Pachana:	Yelled Miss Patricia.
Teacher:	So you see, if I change the expression in my voice the saying process is different for each one.

What the teacher knows from her careful planning is that this text will reward the children's enquiries because part of the transformation of the family setting is achieved through the patterning of saying processes. So she encourages them to search for further examples.

Teacher: But first of all let's read *Piggybook* and find out if we can see
any saying processes. Soon as you hear one could you tell me
and put your hands up?
[*reads*] Mr Piggott lived with his two sons, Simon and Patrick,
in a nice house with a nice garden, and a nice car, in a nice
garage. Inside the house was his wife.
Pachana?

Pachana: And.

Teacher: Did you hear a saying word there? . . . Did anyone say anything
there?

Children: No.

Teacher: No.
[*reads*] 'Hurry up with the breakfast, dear,' he called every
morning.
What's the saying process there? . . . Angelica?

Angelica: 'Called.'

Teacher: 'Called.' Very good.

Pachana's response 'and' is particularly interesting. At this early stage she
obviously does not perceive the differences in structure to which the
teacher is attempting to draw her attention. Her answer demonstrates just
how new the task of attending to structural features of the language is for
at least some of the children. Obviously they are not simply labelling what
they already in some sense know, but rather they are at the very first point
of attending to new, complex phenomena through the use of the metalanguage in the discussion of text in context. The moment is of some
theoretical interest because it is often remarked that children's study of
grammar merely enables them to label concepts about language that they
already have implicitly. That does not appear to be so here, nor in many
other examples of the children's discussions in this group. I argue that the
kind of metalanguage used in these initial moments is very important for
the kinds of discriminations about language that children are eventually
able to make, contrary to the view that the metalanguage is simply grafted
onto concepts which derive from elsewhere. In particular, a functional
description enables a teacher to use the children's understanding of the
meaning features to begin building an understanding of the structural
features. When the problem of distinguishing the saying process occurs the
teacher does not respond by providing a definition but instead uses the
text as a resource to help the children construct their knowledge. (Imagine
if she had first told the children that a verb is a 'doing word'. Even in this
small stretch of language there is the immediate problem of 'was', which is
a verb but not a 'doing word', and 'garden' and 'garage' which are often
used as 'doing words' but are not verbs here.) Angelica's comment enables
the group to refocus its attention in this supportive textual environment,

and then it is only a short time before they can begin to discriminate saying processes and to see how different examples encode a variety of meanings relevant to the representation of character in *Piggybook*.

Teacher:	[*reading*] They never washed the dishes, they never washed their clothes. Soon the house was like a *pigsty.
Children:	*pigsty [*reading with the teacher*]
Teacher:	'When is Mum coming home?' the boys squealed.
Teacher:	Karen?
Karen:	'Squealed.'
Teacher 2:	Mm. 'Squealed.' That's an . . . That's an interesting one. Because . . . what kinds of animals squeal? . . . Paul?
Paul:	Pigs.
Teacher 2:	Yes. So now when Mr Piggott and the boys say things who do they sound like? [*inaudible: child's name*]
Child:	Pigs.
Teacher 2:	Mm. They're starting to sound like pigs as well as acting like pigs. Let's see if we can pick some more of those.

Then it is a relatively simple move to encourage the children to engage in reading with appropriate voice qualities – providing the text with a tune, as it were:

Teacher:	'How should I know?' Mr Piggott grunted. [*lengthy pause*]
Sean:	'Grunted.'
Joan:	'Grunted.' And is that another one that sounds like a pig?
Children:	Yes. . . .
Teacher:	If you were Mr Piggott how would you say that? 'How should I know.' Who can say that? Who can say it in a grunting voice? Jonathan?
Jonathan:	How should I know? [*snorts on 'know', follows by grunting*]

So the children continue, now with a lot of laughter as they experiment further with finding saying processes and reading the quoted language appropriately.

As we have discussed these observations with colleagues some of them have wondered if the children would eventually be able to discriminate the verbs independently as elements of grammatical structure, rather than rely on the specific features of the semantics of an individual text. Our evidence across the project suggests that they can do so, and this includes evidence from independent tests of knowledge of structure. Even in these first moments with the six-year-olds, the move to a more decontextualised understanding of structure came quite quickly, as is clear in the following excerpt.

Teacher:	[*reading*] One night there was nothing in the house for them to cook. 'We'll just have to root around and find some scraps', snorted Mr Piggott.

Danielle:	Oh ah.
Teacher:	Danielle?
Danielle:	'Snorted.'
Teacher:	'Snorted.'
Teacher:	And is that another one that sounds like a pig?
Children:	Yes.
Teacher 2:	Maybe someone could say that one, Miss Patricia? [*writes on chart*]
Teacher:	Oh I think I'll ask Elise.
Elise:	That's a 'ed' word.
Teacher:	Oh, an 'ed' word.

It is a relatively small move from this comment to observing the same feature in many of the saying processes they have identified, and of course then back to the function of the feature in what one hopes would be a continuing dialogue between their observations and the development of more refined understandings of structure.

Evidence of this general kind, together with those from observation of the learning of two groups of older children, has suggested to me that functionally oriented grammatical description is accessible to young children, and that studying language in this way is enjoyable. But was the work of these six-year-olds associated with any observable development in literacy and other use of language?

The answer is clearly yes, with a proviso. In the opinion of teachers who are responsible for this aspect of the curriculum the children's knowledge of functional grammar was associated with greater reading fluency than that of their peers. The children were also able to control the orthographic conventions of speech marks much more readily than their age peers, and better than children two years older in this school. This is not surprising if one considers the likely difference in their understanding of the function of the conventions. Perhaps most interestingly, there is evidence that children played spontaneously with their new metalinguistic learning, just as they had played with language itself in learning how it worked in new fields of experience. This play was evident both in school and at home, according to their parents' observations.

The proviso is that so far it has only been possible to study relatively short-term learning. Clearly what is now needed is comparison of learning outcomes over several years, a phase of the research which we are currently planning.

Some interesting longer-term evidence about the level of abstract understanding children can achieve is, however, available from a group we have studied for two years. These children were initially part of one of the eleven-year-old groups, who elected to continue studying grammar in an after-school club in the subsequent year. The initiative for this move came from the children themselves, who by this time had moved to several different secondary schools. They asked if they could return to their old primary school to continue their study of functional grammar with their teacher, Ruth French, and with me.

At one stage of their work late in the year, the children became interested in the relational verb 'be'. In particular, we discussed differences between 'be' when it indicates a relationship between a member of a class and that broader class (the attributive form), and 'be' when it indicates an identity relation (the identifying form). The difference, for example, between 'Roald Dahl is an author' and 'Roald Dahl is the best author of funny rhyming couplets'. In the former example 'Roald Dahl' is a member of a larger set, one of many authors. In the latter case there is an equivalence relation, where one term becomes the indicator or signifier of the meaning given by the other term. Halliday, in *An Introduction to Functional Grammar* (1994: 119 ff.), calls these Token and Value respectively. In the example, 'Roald Dahl' is the Token and 'the best author of funny rhyming couplets' is the Value. It is a fairly complex region of grammar–meaning relations. However, here is Tamilselvan, now aged twelve, talking with me about some examples. We had been discussing various types of process, then the conversation shifted to the more detailed distinction between attributive and identifying types of relational processes.

Geoff:	'Triceratops was a rather small dinosaur'.
Tamilselvan:	Relational.
Geoff:	OK. So now maybe can we go down into another level of description and say what kind of relationals they are?
Tamilselvan:	Um.
Geoff:	So if we take them just turn by turn.
Tamilselvan:	Such as identifying?
Geoff:	Yeah. Identifying or attributive were the two we did. Can you remember or can you work out . . . say . . . Let's take this one first of all. Let's just leave that one. 'Tyrannosaurus rex was extremely large.'
Tamilselvan:	Um that . . . that would be attributive.
Geoff:	And why? . . . Why would you say that?
Tamilselvan:	Ah . . . well umm . . . if we go by the fact that identifying you can switch it around. [*He is here using a test of equivalence we had introduced some time before.*]
Geoff:	Mm.
Tamilselvan:	You can switch the two sides around like . . .
Geoff:	Right, right.
Tamilselvan:	You wouldn't normally say 'Extremely large was tyrannosaurus'. Um I mean you could but it doesn't sound too . . .
Geoff:	It's unlikely, isn't it?

(There was a short break while I attended to an interruption.)

Geoff: What about 'tyrannosaurus rex was carnivorous'?
Tamilselvan: Again attributive.
Geoff: And then let's go back up to this one 'The largest of the dinosaurs was tyrannosaurus rex.'
Tamilselvan: I think that would be an identified that would be identifying because um 'Tyrannosaurus rex was the largest of the dinosaurs.'
Geoff: Mm. Good, thanks. And this one 'Triceratops was a rather small dinosaur.'
Tamilselvan: Um. Attributive, I think.

A little later we discussed the further distinction in the identifying form between the elements Token and Value.

Geoff: Do you remember the terms Token and Value that we had a couple of weeks ago?
Tamilselvan: Yes.
Geoff: 'Tyrannosaurus rex' and 'the largest of the dinosaurs'. So one's going to be Token and one's going to be Value.
Tamilselvan: Well um 'Tyrannosaurus rex' is the Token, right? And 'the largest of the dinosaurs' is the Value.

He continued to make these distinctions accurately in several further examples. Clearly, he has no difficulty in handling these abstract concepts about language, and neither did other children who participated in the same activity.

It would seem, then, that it is not so much the capacities of children which limit possibility for reflection on language in primary schools, but limited community understanding of what a grammar is and therefore an obsessive preoccupation with the mythical educative qualities of traditional grammar. It is more than time to begin to reimagine possibilities for explicit, systematic language study in primary schools beyond the confines of traditional school grammar, unrelated as it has become to meaning. My view, deriving from the research data from which I've been illustrating, is that it is just as possible for many children to have the same sense of excitement about entering the abstract world of meta-reflection on language as they have when they first begin to read and write successfully.

Variation in literate practices in families in relation to school practices

The third major aspect which a perspective from textual practices illuminates is variation in literacy practices in contemporary communities. Given that it is such a large and complex topic, my purposes here are restricted to indicating some lines of enquiry in order particularly to critique the rela-tions introduced in figure 2.2 and to suggest broadly how literacy learning difficulties might be re-imagined from a linguistic perspective.

Media discussions of children's literacy problems in school make dealing with literacy problems in the first few years of school simply a matter of more work on the 'fundamentals', by which is usually meant phonics. So insistent is this assertion that political parties in various English-speaking countries are legislating the presence of phonics programmes in early literacy education as a *general* remedy for children's literacy difficulties. It is one thing to determine that children should be 'phonemically aware', to use the current vogue term, and that they should be provided with systematic instruction to build this awareness as needed, but quite another to assert that instruction in phonics is a necessary and sufficient condition for success in school literacy. One consequence of this view is that when some children continue to experience literacy difficulties the problem is treated as an individual one: tragic, but individual.

What can now be sketched in, at least in broad outline from transdisci-plinary work on literacy is that often the problem is not individual but social. This is a common claim, so I should be careful to specify what I mean here by social. I mean social not only in the sense of effects of social relations in school, or even of differences between home dialect and that of the school, nor of differences between home language and English. Rather, I mean social in the very deep sense of effects of social structure on language use, and therefore on literacy practices within different social locations.

For the study of early literacy development specifically, some interesting evidence comes from research concerning joint book-reading practices at home and in the first year of school. Heath (1983), for example, in studying three contrasted communities in the south-east of the United States, found marked differences in uses of reading and writing. The contrast is not one of different degrees or qualities of literacy, but rather of variable literate practices, particularly evident in parents' discussions of narrative texts with preschoolers. Wells, too, in his well-known Bristol study of factors associated with precocious literacy development found important variation in family practices (Wells, 1985). In a Sydney study in which intensive linguistic analyses were made of transcripts of recordings of intact sessions of joint book-reading, Williams (1995) found significant variation in a range of language practices associated with participants' social class locations. This study also analysed transcripts of joint book-reading during the first few months of children's schooling and found a marked similarity between the typical practices of the middle-class family group and that of the kindergarten teachers.[2]

What is this similarity? It is many-faceted, but here is an example of one feature. Variation is evident in an expectation that children should make linguistically explicit the bases of their judgements and interpretations. In some families occasions for talking about the most familiar of stories can be a context for the expectation to play its part in interaction. In others, children are rarely if ever asked to make explicit what can, after all, readily be taken for granted since the story is so familiar. In the following excerpt Rachel and her mother are reading and discussing *The Three Little Pigs*. It is evident from comments made early in their conversation that this is a story they have read together many times before. Nevertheless her mother uses the occasion to get Rachel to explicate her reasoning in ways other families would find distinctly puzzling.

Mother: [*reading*] So slap, slosh, slap away he worked laying bricks and smoothing mortar between them.
            What's that?
Rachel: A wolf.
Mother: Isn't it a puppy dog?
Rachel: It's a wolf.
Mother: You sure?
Rachel: Look at his sharp teeth . . . that doesn't look like . . . Look at it. See it standing up?
Mother: What's standing up?
Rachel: Look.
Mother: Do wolves walk on their back legs, do they?
Rachel: Yes.
Mother: Oh. Why don't they walk on four legs like a puppy dog?
Rachel: 'Cause they don't have they don't have um they don't have dogs or things the same . . . only all of the dogs.
Mother: Mm?
Rachel: Only all of the dogs.
Mother: They look like a dog's head.

There is a strong sense of apprenticeship to this reasoning since it is a form of discourse which Rachel obviously doesn't yet control. Nevertheless she is evidently engaged by it since she returns to the problem a short while later.

Rachel: No. Look at . . . They look like their ears.
Mother: Yeah, they've got ears like a dog. Do wolves only walk on their back legs, do they?
Rachel: They haven't got that big mouth.
Mother: Dogs do. And they've got sharp teeth like that.
Rachel: I know. Well they . . . well they well they don't . . . they don't . . . they don't eat they don't eat pigs.
Mother: Oh I see.
Rachel: They eat bones. They have bones.

Mother: Dogs eat bones and wolves eat pigs. Is that right?
[*resuming reading*] 'Ha, ha, ha,' laughed the first little pig.

It would be very difficult to argue that there is *inherently* anything good about such discussions, but there is little doubt that certain features are typical of discourse in schools and in just one fraction of the community, at least in so far as children are required to explicate and justify their reasoning about textual phenomena. Children for whom these practices are unfamiliar have therefore not just to learn about grapheme–phoneme relations as they enter school literacy. They have also to understand both the nature of unfamiliar literate activity and what is required of them in speaking in those activities. It is a matter both of recognising the type of context and how to speak within it, to paraphrase the important theoretical point about contextual variation which Bernstein makes in his discussion of differences in coding orientation (Bernstein, 1990, 1996). This is, as I remarked above, just one instance of the more general variation evident in studies of joint book-reading, and also in larger-scale studies of children learning through casual conversation in the home and the first year of schooling (Hasan, 1989, 1991, 1992; Hasan and Cloran, 1990).

In overview what this evidence necessitates is a considerable modification of figure 2.2, to take account of the influence of social location and different mediating practices in the ontogenesis of literacy. Something like figure 2.4 might be a starting point into which details must be sketched. The model suggests not only variation between children in social location and variation in textual practices, but also that processes of reading and writing will themselves be differently realised as a result of these variations in textual practices. What is needed in early literacy pedagogy is a much more detailed understanding of what children construe reading and writing to be through the mediating influence of the textual practices in which they participate. It is an urgent further task for linguistically informed classroom research, in dialogue with powerful sociological theory of social structure.

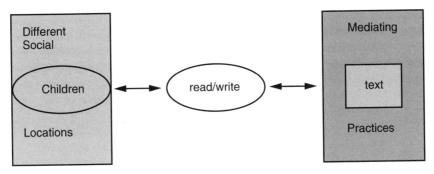

Figure 2.4 An elaborated model of reading as interactive process in social contexts

Concluding comments

Thinking about literacy development in terms of entry to textual practices, though it is a hugely complex task, does offer means to broaden over-familiar perspectives, dependent as they are on images of a return to mythical fundamentals of written language and its description. It also provides a basis for a positive view of children's capacities to understand literate practices. In fact, if I were to have to nominate the single most important limitation on children's literacy development it would be this: adults' restricted expectations for what children are capable of under-standing about language and its use as text. Changes to these expectations are, I think, amongst our best hopes for supporting children's entry into an increasingly complex range of literate worlds.

Notes

1   For related discussion see Chambers, A. 1985. 'The reader in the book'. In *Booktalk. Occasional Writing on Literature and Children.* London: Bodley Head; Stephens, J. 1992. *Language and Ideology in Children's Fiction.* London: Longman. Eco advances some reasons for a linguistically based sense of a model reader.
2   For further discussion see Williams, G. in press. 'The pedagogic device and the production of pedagogic discourse: a case example in early literacy education'. In F. Christie (ed.), *Pedagogy and the Shaping of Consciousness: Linguistic and Social Processes.* London: Cassell Academic.

References

Austin, J. 1961. *Sense and Sensibility,* New York: Harper and Row.
Baillie, A. and Tanner, J. 1988. *Drac and the Gremlin.* South Yarra, Viking Kestrel.
Bernstein, B. 1990. *The Structuring of Pedagogic Discourse. Class, Codes and control,* Volume 4. London, Routledge and Kegan Paul.
—— 1996. *Pedagogy, Symbolic Control and Identity: Theory, Research, Critique.* London, Taylor and Francis.
Browne, A. 1983. *Gorilla.* London, Julia MacRae Books.
—— 1986. *Piggybook.* London, Julia MacRae Books.
Carter, R. 1996. 'Politics and knowledge about language: the LINC Project'. In R. Hasan and G. Williams (eds) *Literacy in Society.* London, Addison-Wesley Longman.
Chambers, A. 1985. *Booktalk: Occasional Writing on Literature and Children.* London, The Bodley Head.
Christie, F. 1990. 'Curriculum genre in early childhood education: a case study in writing development'. Ph.D. Thesis. Department of Linguistics, University of Sydney.
Chukovsky, K. 1968. *From Two to Five.* revised edn. Trans. and Ed. M. Morton. Berkeley and London, University of California Press.

Eco, U. 1995. *Six Walks in the Fictional Woods*. Cambridge, Mass., Harvard University Press.

Fox, C. 1993. *At the Very Edge of the Forest: The Influence of Literature on Storytelling by Children*. London, Cassell.

Halliday, M. A. K. 1975. *Learning How to Mean: Explorations in the Development of Language*. London, Edward Arnold.

—— 1994. *An Introduction to Functional Grammar*. second edn. London, Edward Arnold.

Hasan, R. 1985. *Linguistics, Language and Verbal Art*. Geelong, Deakin University Press.

—— 1989. 'Semantic variation and sociolinguistics'. In *Australian Journal of Linguistics*. 9. pp. 221–75.

—— 1991. 'Questions as a mode of learning in everyday talk'. In T. Le and M. McCausland (eds) *Language Education: Interaction and Development*. Proceedings of the International Conference held in Ho Chi Minh City, Vietnam, 30 March–1 April 1991. Launceston, University of Tasmania.

—— 1992. 'Meaning in sociolinguistic theory'. In K. Bolton and H. Kwok (eds) *Sociolinguistics Today: International Perspectives*. London and New York, Routledge.

Hasan, R. and Cloran, C. 1990. 'A sociolinguistic interpretation of everyday talk between mothers and children.' In M. A. K. Halliday, J. Gibbons and H. Nicholas (eds) *Learning, Keeping and Using Language*. Selected papers from the 8th World Congress of Applied Linguistics, Sydney, 16–21 August 1987. Amsterdam/Philadelphia, John Benjamins Publishing Company.

Heath, S. B. 1983. *Ways With Words: Language, Life and Work in Communities and Classrooms*. Cambridge, Cambridge University Press.

Kress, G. and van Leeuwen, T. 1990. *Reading Images*. Geelong, Deakin University Press.

—— 1996. *Reading Images: The Grammar of Visual Design*. London, Routledge.

Machin, S. and Vivas, J. 1989. *I Went Walking*. Norwood, Omnibus Books.

Matthiessen, C. M. M. 1996. *Lexicogrammatical Cartography: English Systems*. Tokyo, International Language Science Publishers.

Meek, M. 1988. *How Texts Teach What Readers Learn*. Stroud, The Thimble Press.

Mukarovsky, J. 1977. *The Word and Verbal Art*. Trans. J. Burbank and P. Steiner. New Haven, Yale University Press.

Painter, C. 1996. 'The development of language as a resource for thinking'. In R. Hasan and G. Williams (eds) *Literacy in Society*. London, Addison-Wesley Longman.

Sendak, M. 1967. *Where the Wild Things Are*. London, The Bodley Head.

Stephens, J. 1992. *Language and Ideology in Children's Fiction*. London, Longman.

Vygotsky, L. 1981. 'The genesis of higher mental functions'. In J. V. Wertsch (ed.) *The Concept of Activity in Soviet Psychology*. New York, M. E. Sharpe.

—— 1986. *Thought and Language*. Trans. and Ed. A. Kozulin. Cambridge, Mass. and London, The MIT Press.

Wells, C. G. 1985. 'Pre-school literacy-related activities and success in school'. In D. R. Olson, N. Torrance and A. Hildyard. (eds) *Literacy, Language and*

Learning: The Nature and Consequences of Reading and Writing. Cambridge, Cambridge University Press.

Williams, G. 1995. 'Joint book-reading and literacy pedagogy: a socio-semantic examination.' Volume 1. CORE. 19(3). Fiche 2 B01-Fiche 6 B01.

—— in press. 'The pedagogic device and the production of pedagogic discourse: a case example in early literacy education.' In F. Christie (ed.) *Pedagogy and the Shaping of Consciousness: Linguistic and Social Processes*. London, Cassell Academic.

3

Learning the literacies of primary and secondary schooling

Frances Christie

Introduction

There are at least two myths abroad in literacy education, the one having quite an old history, the other being much more recent in its origins. The first, and older of the two myths (whose origins are in fact some centuries old), is that which holds that the learning of literacy is a particular, even a unique, task for the first years of schooling. Learning to read and write is a matter primarily of mastering the spelling, handwriting and punctuation systems, and hence of being able both to make meaning of the words on the printed page, and to construct meanings oneself by writing. The teacher's role in this view of things, is to focus in particular on teaching these systems, often indeed at the cost of sense and meaning, so insistent can the demand be to teach and reinforce such things as a sense of sound–letter correspondence. The second myth, dating in particular from the 1970s and 1980s, is that which proposes that the learning of literacy is a 'natural' process, and that it is learned in much the same way as is speech. In the model proposed in this case, the teacher's role is to be at best supporter and facilitator as children develop skills with literacy in largely untutored ways.

Both myths are harmful, distorting what are in fact much more complex issues and processes. To take the former myth, we can see that involved here is a conventional view of literacy, as being essentially constructed in writing, spelling and punctuation. Like many other myths, this one has some elements of truth, although it does not do justice to the true situation. English orthography, handwriting and punctuation are very important, especially in the first years of schooling, and where students attempt to proceed up the years of school while still experiencing difficulties in control of these matters, they run into trouble. However, spelling, punctuation and handwriting are also the most visible manifestations of literate behaviour, and it is for that reason very easy to be persuaded that mastery of these things represents the sum total of appropriate literate behaviour. The sum total, as we shall see, is infinitely more complex, involving mastery of the grammatical features of written, as opposed to spoken language, but these features, regrettably, are often not very apparent.

To turn to the second of the myths, this derives from the influence of writers such as Goodman (1982) and also Smith (e.g. 1985), both of whom commenced their writing in the late 1960s and 1970s, and both of whom were influenced by the linguistic theories of Chomsky (though it is notable that Chomsky has never claimed any educational relevance for his theories). Both subscribed to the view that the ability to learn language is innate, and that observation of the ways oral language is learned by normal children encourages the view that they proceed by processes of trial and error to identify the rules by which language is put together and used.[1] The view went on to propose that literacy is best learned in the same ways as speech, and that too much overt intervention on the part of the teacher can be a cause of harm. For Goodman (cited by Reid, 1993: 23) at least, reading was seen as 'the direct counterpart' of listening, and learned in the same 'natural' way. In a paper Goodman gave at the Regional Language Centre Seminar on 'Reading and Writing: Theory into Practice' in Singapore in 1994, he argued a similar view of the learning of writing: it parallels the learning of speech, and should be allowed to develop in 'natural' and untutored ways.[2]

Just as there is an element of truth in the older myth, there is at least some truth in the 'natural' learning theories of Goodman, Smith and others. First-hand observation of children, apart from the wealth of available research evidence about how children learn their mother tongue, makes it clear that engagement in normal everyday activities with caregivers provides the best – and therefore most 'natural' way for children to learn language. Hence – and many good teachers can attest to this – children learn literacy best in ways that provide opportunities to learn and understand it for mean- ingful and rewarding purposes, so that these too may be understood as 'natural'. But for all that, 'natural' learning theories are in fact very barren, because they fail to grasp both how different written language is from speech, and how critical is the role of the teacher in intervening to teach students literacy.

Where, as in the former myth, it is the view that literate behaviour is all about spelling, punctuation and the writing system, there are at least two unfortunate consequences in educational practice. First, there is an assump- tion that everything children need to know about being literate should be mastered by about age eight or nine. In this view, literacy is uni-dimen- sional. The view holds that some essential skills for reading and writing are established in the early years, and the implication beyond that is that, in some very unproblematic way, these skills get recycled ever after as students grow older, moving up the years of schooling and entering adult life. The second and related unfortunate consequence of the assumption that literacy is all about spelling, writing and punctuation, is that it deskills teachers; it causes them not to acknowledge or to teach for a developing understanding of the nature of literacy, and of the ways it changes, both as students grow older, and as they encounter and deal with different kinds of knowledge and experience. The truth is that literacy is multi-dimensional, not uni-dimensional, that there are many literate practices, and that the learning of literacy takes many years. (See Macken-Horarik and Williams in this volume for related discussions.) Indeed, it can be argued that the learning of literacy is lifelong. Particularly in the contemporary world, and under the pressures of developments in information technology (see Morgan, Lankshear and Knobel, this volume), there is reason to believe that literacy is undergoing frequent rapid change, causing all of us to work at understanding its new potential and possibilities.

As for the second myth, I have already suggested something of its harmful consequences. First, in that the view of language and learning here assumes that written language is learned in the same way as speech, it fails to acknowledge just how different the two modes of using language really are. It therefore has nothing useful to say about the features of written language, and leaves teachers and students alike uninformed. Second, in that the view assumes the benefits of a facilitative rather than an interventionist role on the part of the teacher, this also deskills the teacher, encouraging a sense that there is no expert knowledge to be offered students as they learn literacy.

While the two myths identified have had different historical and theoretical bases, I shall suggest in this chapter that the two are alike in that both hold very limited models of the nature of language generally, and of literacy learning in particular, across the years of schooling. I shall argue that if we adopt a functional model of language and literacy, we can actually trace linguistic evidence for some of the significant milestones in literacy learning that need to occur throughout the years of schooling if students are to emerge with a reasonable degree of proficiency. Additionally, we can suggest something of the knowledge teachers will require in order to teach literacy properly across the years of school.

In order to develop the argument here, I propose to examine below some of the most rudimentary of the texts young children learn to write, and then go on to examine a sampling of those by older students. One might of course, develop a similar or complementary argument by reference to the text types, or genres, students need to read at different stages of their learning. One reason examination of writing is particularly revealing, however, is that it is the productive mode: it reveals something of the actual tasks in composing literate texts that students have to handle in their learning.

First, however, before I commence examination of a selection of written text types or genres across the years of schooling, I want to offer some general observations about spoken and written language, and about the kinds of knowledge that schooling requires students increasingly to handle with respect to literacy. I shall also make some observations about the values of a functional grammar as a tool for exploring the nature of language, spoken and written. I shall suggest that the nature of literacy changes as students grow older, and that there is a relationship between the changing patterns of written language that students need to recognise and use, and the varieties of knowledge they need to learn. A functional grammar, I shall suggest, allows us to trace features of the changes.

Spoken and written language

A variety of twentieth-century research, by linguists (e.g. Halliday, 1975, 1985), psychologists (e.g. Vygotsky, 1962; Luria, 1976; Trevarthen, 1987; Bruner, 1986), anthropologists (e.g. Malinowski, 1923; Goody, 1968) palaeoanthropologists (e.g. Leakey, 1994) and sociologists (e.g. Berger and Luckman, 1966; Bernstein, 1975) has testified to the great significance of language in all human communities. Oral language is the basic resource with which individuals grow and express their identity as well as participate in and comprehend their social groups.

With the advent of literacy humans learned to handle experience in new ways. The greatest change that literacy afforded involved a distancing effect. Both the writer and the reader became distanced from the events and/or information recorded in writing. Thus, events and/or information could be recorded and communicated to persons who were distant over space – say in another region or another country – and over time – say in future unborn generations. To handle information in either sense is to do things differently from the way they are done in speech. Thus, for example, whenever we take events lived and talked about in the immediacy of face-to-face interaction, and reconstruct these for an audience in another time or place, we change the events. We represent them differently, drawing upon graphic means to do so, employing a writing system and a spelling system in the process. In addition, we change the grammatical choices in which we represent the events. That is to say, we build knowledge of the events in new ways.

As Halliday (1985) has suggested, we need to be careful about drawing too neat a parallel between the processes by which humans evolved their languages and subsequently their written modes and the processes by which children learn their mother tongue and thence learn literacy. Evolution is not the same as growth in learning. Nevertheless, there is a sense in which certain parallels apply. Thus, for most children the first steps in becoming literate appear to emerge from prior efforts in drawing, just as it seems the world's writing systems evolved from earlier experiences in drawing and painting.

Early childhood teachers often encourage children to do drawings and to write about them. One young child in the preparatory or kindergarten year produced a picture of himself and family at the beach, and produced a rudimentary script. The teacher wrote what she understood to be Mark's meanings beneath, referring to his 'beach towel' (see figure 3.1). The little script is of interest for several reasons. My principal interest here lies in the fact that the child, quite unable to write the words 'beach towel', actually drew a little picture of one, taking its place on the line in what otherwise constitutes a reasonably good attempt to produce written English. He had produced an ideograph. But the general character of the rest of the piece shows he knew he was employing not the semiotic system of drawing, but that of writing. In a study of the early writing development of about fifty-five children over the first three years of their schooling (Christie, 1989), this child was the only one ever to produce such a script with ideograph. It would seem to be uncommon. Herein lies important evidence to suggest that children fairly early learn that drawing and writing are different, and that they achieve different ends. Where drawing represents actual things such as a beach towel, writing represents language. Writing is a symbolic system of a different order from drawing.

Developing proficiency with control of the symbolic system of writing requires that students engage increasingly with the grammatical features of the written mode. However, the processes of learning the grammar of

Figure 3.1 Mark's drawing

writing take several years. Indeed, the evidence (e.g. Halliday, 1994; Derewianka, 1996; Christie, 1995a, b, c, 1996, 1997) would suggest that control of written language is a development of late childhood and early adolescence, though the pattern varies a great deal with individuals. As the grammar of written language changes, so too do the kinds of knowledge that students are asked to learn.

In the early days and years of schooling, a great deal of what is learned relies upon manipulation of what we will call 'commonsense' knowledge: the knowledge of the familiar and the commonplace, of what is known and observed in family and community. Good early childhood teachers actively exploit knowledge of these matters as, for example, they teach children about such things as good foods to eat (aspects of the school health programme), the passage of the seasons (aspects of the natural science programme), or movement about the streets , including use of safe crossings and traffic lights (aspects of the social science programme), where in all cases, familiar everyday experience provides a commonsense knowledge for teaching and learning. The first writing experiences of young children deal with the familiar and the commonsense, but as students grow older they move increasingly into learning 'un-commonsense' knowledge (Bernstein, 1975): i.e. knowledge that is esoteric in some sense, and not familiarly available.

Un-commonsense knowledge is not a fixed commodity, as it tends to vary in different periods of history: what is commonsense today may well have been un-commonsense in an earlier time. But what is clear is that learning un-commonsense knowledge is effortful, it tends to take time and it normally requires some assistance in its mastery. Such knowledge, while of course often freely talked about, is typically also found in patterns of written language, which by their nature are quite different from the early patterns of commonsense knowledge construction.

Bearing these observations in mind we will examine some instances of written language, initially from the early years of schooling, and then from the later years. Before I commence this discussion, however, I want to say a little of the systemic functional grammar (e.g. Halliday, 1994; Martin, 1992a; Matthiessen, 1995) and associated theories of register and genre used to examine the texts.

Systemic functional grammar, register and genre

There are currently around the world various functional approaches to language studies, and several might well be used to address educational questions. Systemic functional (SF) grammar is distinctive in several senses, and it is because of these that I shall make some selective use of the grammar here. SF grammar has a reasonably well-established history of involvement in education, having been drawn upon in a number of educational projects and reports in the UK (it was drawn upon by Carter and others, for example, in developing the Language in the National Curriculum Project) and in Australia (Christie *et al.*, 1991. See Christie, 1991 and Martin, 1992b for some representative discussions of the ways SF theory has been used to inform language education developments in Australia.) It is partly because the grammar has such an established history of involvement in educational theory and research that I draw on it here: it has a track record.

One of the most distinctive of the features of SF grammar is its claim that all natural languages have three major *metafunctions:* the *ideational* (to do with the experiences, or the 'content' represented in language), the *interpersonal* (to do with the nature of the relationship of the participants involved in using language) and the *textual* (to do with the manner in which sequences of language items 'hang together' to build meanings and hence create texts). When we use language, we select from the total language system those items necessary: to achieve our goals in representing some aspect(s) of experience or information, to construct and/or negotiate our relationships with others, and to build meaningful text.

The particular language choices we make at any time depend in part on the *context of situation* and the *register* associated with it, and partly on the *context of culture* and the associated *genre.* Some examples will suffice to demonstrate the point. In the course of a typical day, the average person will move into many different contexts of situation. Assume a typical day in the life of a teacher who, on leaving home in the morning, stops at the local garage to buy petrol, holding a conversation with the petrol vendor, then travels to school, where she chairs a curriculum planning meeting with other teachers, receives a telephone conversation from a concerned parent about a child, teaches several lessons to different classes, and writes several reports on curriculum matters. Each of the different activities just sketched in represents a different context of situation, requiring different language choices with respect to register. That is to say, interpersonally, the teacher assumes a different relationship with the other participants involved in each context of situation; ideationally, she deals with different experiences or information; while textually, sometimes she engages in face-to-face conversation, sometimes (as in the case of the phone conversation) she holds conversation with an unseen participant, and sometimes (as in the reports) she produces written text for a relatively remote audience. All these subtle shifts with respect to register are known, or are realised, in the different language choices the teacher takes up.

Since the imagined teacher is assumed to be in an English-speaking context of culture, we can expect that the genres involved are all those characteristic of English-speaking cultures. A genre, as the term is used here, is a staged, purposeful, goal-directed activity represented in language. The trade encounter with the petrol vendor (see Ventola, 1987 and Hasan, 1985 for analyses of related genres), for example, will be one representative instance of a genre, while the lessons will constitute 'curriculum genres' (e.g. Christie, 1995a, b, c, 1996, 1997), or perhaps parts of such genres, where they could embrace several lessons. The telephone conversation, the meeting procedure, the written reports will all have distinctive genres: a distinctive series of stages through which the participant(s) must move in order to achieve the goals of the activities involved.

To this point, the only terms I have used from the SF grammar referred to the three metafunctions. Below, as I examine a representative sample of written texts produced by students across the years of schooling, I shall, as appropriate, introduce other terms taken from the SF grammar to describe particular language choices. Two matters should be noted; first, on occasion I shall use terms that will be known to readers familiar with more traditional models of grammar, for many are retained in the functional description; second, a full SF description will not be attempted with respect to any text.

Early writing behaviour

Necessarily, language is learned in face-to-face interaction, and the patterns of speech reflect and reveal much of the immediacy of the ways in which language is used. As noted above, the particular achievement of writing is that it enables people to use language for other than the immediate context of face-to-face interaction: it affords a distancing from the matters written about in terms of time and space. It is these particular distancing features that, more than anything else, account for the grammatical differences between speech and writing.[3] Young children of course understand nothing of this, and it takes some years for a consciousness of the grammatical features of written, as opposed to spoken language to emerge.

A child in Year 1 wrote the following (spelling corrected), which is set out to reveal the two clauses involved:

I'm going to see a kangaroo and a koala
but I found my mum and my dad.

Technically, this piece does not qualify as a text, since while it is certainly English, it is difficult to see that the two clauses cohere to create the unity we should expect in a text. Plainly, the young writer uses fragments of personal experience, but without advice about the context(s) from which the child draws the experience, the meaning of the sentence is not clear. Had it been possible to speak to the child, it would no doubt have been possible to retrieve the connections he intended between his apparently disparate clauses. But the opportunity afforded for clarification in speech is not so readily available once one has embarked on use of the written mode. In an important sense, written language removes its experience from the immediacy of the face-to-face interaction, bringing about changes in the grammar which children find hard to grasp.

As students grow a little older and learn to write at more sustained lengths, they produce texts such as the following (with spelling corrected), which I have set out clause by clause to reveal something of its grammatical organisation:

Text 1 Anakie Gorge[*]

On Wednesday we went to Anakie Gorge[4]
and «**when** we went» we went past Fairy Park
and «**when** we got there» we walked down the path
and we saw a koala
and we saw a lizard
and there was dead foxes hanging on the fence
and we walked on to the picnic place
and then we climbed up the mountain
and I nearly slipped
so I went down
and « **when** everyone was down» we had lunch
and then we went for a walk to the creek
and found stones
and boys were throwing stones in the water
and «**when** we were coming back» Jeffrey fell in the creek
and «**before** we went» we made daisy chains. The End.

The writer of Text 1 narrates personal experience, creating what Rothery (1984) termed a recount. The most distinctive features of such a text are:

- the fact that it recreates personal experience and activities, evident in part in the extensive use of personal pronouns, and also in the many material processes, such as 'we went', 'we got there', 'we walked'. (The functional grammar, identifies different types of processes realised in verbs and their associated participants.)[5]
- its overt and frequent uses of conjunctive relations (marked in bold) to link the clauses through which she reconstructs personal experience;
- the very strong sense of additive connection established in these conjunctive relations;
- the use of the past tense indicating the writer is aware she is reconstructing past events.

The text succeeds as a piece of coherent written language, though it makes few

---

[*]   The symbols « » indicate a clause that is said to be enclosed within another. Thus the clause 'when we went' is enclosed within 'and we went past Fairy Park'.

uses of punctuation. For all that, the text is grammatically closer to speech than to mature writing. The reason we can say this is that it strings together a sequence of clauses, overtly linked through uses of conjunctions as already noted, in a manner more characteristic of talk than of writing. The tendency of written language, as opposed to speech, as we shall see later, is to compress independent clauses, often burying the conjunctive relations found between clauses, and re-expressing the information in different grammatical choices.

Another early text type is that found in Text 2.

Text 2 How to make chocolate eggs

Things we need
water
frying pan
moulds
two bowls
brown and white chocolate

How to make them
1 put water in the frying pan
2 put the bowl in the water in the pan
3 put the frying pan on
4 melt the chocolate
5 put chocolate in the mould
6 put the mould in the fridge
7 tip eggs out of mould
8 put eggs on the plate
9 and eat them.

Text 2 has a lot in common with Text 1. Ideationally, it also draws on personal experience, and it is built round a sequence of steps. Like Text 1, it uses material processes ('put', 'melt, 'tip'), constructing actions in fact. But unlike Text 1, Text 2 does not reconstruct events. Interpersonally, the writer of Text 2 takes up a very different relationship *vis à vis* the reader. Text 2 directs the actions of others in the manner of all procedural genres. Where the declarative mood choice was selected in Text 1 for the building of information, Text 2 selects the imperative mood as an important aspect of constructing its meanings.

Simple recounts and procedures in the manner of Texts 1 and 2 would seem to be prototypical, even elemental genres in an English-speaking culture. It is this more than anything else that must explain the enduring nature of such text types in young learners' classrooms. Recreating event and directing others to action would seem to be two quite fundamental ways of making meaning. Early production of such text types is regularly rehearsed in speech, and this explains for example, the role of morning news or show-and-tell sessions in early childhood education, in which young students often practise narrating events to others, or on occasion they practise telling others how to do something.

But the challenge of learning literacy – indeed a significant challenge of school learning – is learning to handle more than personal experience. As we shall see, learning to deal with the researched experience of a gradually expanding curriculum involves learning to handle language in new ways.

Writing in the middle to upper primary school years

Text 3, by a child of eight years old in Year 3 is an interestingly transitional text, since it certainly recreates personal experience, but it also provides evidence of capacity to make deductions from personal experience, in a manner characteristic of Western scientific endeavour. I am indebted to Aidman (in prep.) who collected the text, for permission to use it here.

Text 3 Science works

Record of Events
One Monday 29th April Grade 3V went to Science works.
We went to a science show.
The lady [[that put on the show]] showed us experiments with liquid nitrogen.
One of them was with a flower.
She put the flower in the liquid nitrogen
and then put it on the table.
The flower died.
She did the same thing to a squash ball
but «when she warmed it up» it went back to normal.

Results
And that shows
that non-living things can go back to normal
but living things cannot
after being put in liquid nitrogen.

Text 3 is an early, if incomplete, example of what Veel (1992), studying science teaching in the junior secondary school, has identified as a 'procedural recount'. It outlines the procedure or set of steps the lady at the science show carried out in the opening element, but then, critically, it concludes with a subsequent element, shown in italics, in which the implications of the simple procedure are indicated. This latter element of its structure is signalled through several linguistic means:

- the use of the conjunction 'and', building connectedness to the earlier element of the genre, but also heralding the start of the new element, where the student writes 'And that shows . . . ';
- the use of the very general referent 'that' in the same clause to refer back in a summary way to the steps in the procedure;
- the use of the verbal or signifying process 'shows' in the same clause signalling that the significance of the events is to be revealed. (See Williams this volume for some discussion of verbal or what he calls 'saying processes'.);
- the shift from the past to the present tense, indicating that the writer adopts a different aspect towards the experience being constructed. The simple present tense choice indicates that the meanings endure, or are in a sense 'timeless'.

The young writer was in fact the only child in her class who wrote such a text type, for none of the others seemed able to write the concluding element in particular. This would suggest that it was for them a difficult thing to do.

The child who wrote Text 3 reproduced the set of steps in which the science lady did her simple experiment in a manner not unlike the young writer who produced Text 2: that is, for each event a separate clause was produced, and the clauses were linked by a conjunctive relation. This is to reproduce experience in a congruent manner: that is to say, for each one step or event, there is one clause to build it. The tendency to reproduce experience this way is the tendency of speech. We string the experiences and events of life together as series of interconnecting clauses, marking their connectedness through frequent use of conjunctive relations. This no doubt makes it easier for our listeners to follow what we are saying than if we produced language closer to true written language. This is not of course to suggest that speech is better than writing, or vice versa. On the contrary, it is to draw attention to the important matter that the two are very different. Written language has evolved over the centuries to do things that speech doesn't do. It necessarily takes many years to master the grammatical organisation of written language. It is not a developmental feature of primary aged children.

Text 4, about the processes by which gold bullion is produced was written by a student in Year 6 of the primary school. It is reproduced here by permission of Sandiford (1988), who collected it in her work with students learning to research and write explanation genres. Once again, I have set it out showing the independent clauses on separate lines, and also marking instances of conjunctive relations in bold. This helps reveal something of the grammatical choices by which the text is put together. The genre has two elements of structure, the opening one in which the phenomenon to be discussed is introduced, and a longer element in which the processes are explained by which that phenomenon comes about. The two elements are labelled, though the student did not write these labels.

Text 4 Gold mining

Phenomenon
Over the years people have thought of many different ways
[[of processing ore]]
to find gold and other precious minerals.
Up to now they used horses and manual strength
but now there is a whole new way [[to process ore]].

Explanation sequence
The process starts
when the ore is blasted from the mine
and brought up to the surface.
The ore is very big
when taken from the mine
so before it can be processed
it has to be crushed.
The first stage [[that the ore goes through]] is 'primary crushing',
when the ore passess through the jaw crusher, the cone crusher
and finally the screen
which only lets particles smaller than 10mm pass.
The small bits of ore are mixed with water
to form a thick mud [[called slurry]].
In the slurry the heavier particles of gold sink to the bottom,
the lighter parts are then washed away.
The slurry passess through a series of chemical treatment(s).
This treatment is necessary
to separate the gold from waste.
The slurry is pumped into a series of 12 tanks.
Air is blown in
and the slurry and chemicals are mixed together under high temperature
in a process [[known as gold leaching.]]
Then gold with some waste is put into a special tank with pieces of
carbon in it.
Gold attaches itself to the carbon.
The carbon with gold is screened out of the tank
and washed with cyanide at high temperatures.
Then an electric current in steel wool attracts the gold particles.
The steel wool is then dissolved into hydrochloric acid
and gold particles are smelted.
Smelting is the last process in gold mining,
which purifies the gold to 99.9% pureness (purity).

Once the gold is pure
it is poured into moulds,
where it cools
and hardens
and becomes gold bullion.

Text 4 shows a student who is dealing with un-commonsense knowledge: knowledge that is, which was quite outside his experience, which required some research to identify it, and which also required some skill in representing that knowledge in a manner that adequately explained the phenomenon. Some linguistic features particularly involved in the construction of such knowledge and such a genre include:

- a number of processes, some of which are material, and involved in building the activities through which the gold is processed (e.g. 'the process starts', 'it can be crushed', 'the slurry is pumped') and several relational processes, involved either in building features of the gold and other elements (e.g. 'the ore is very big') or sometimes in identifying some phenomenon (e.g. 'the first stage [[that the ore goes through]] is "primary crushing"');
- the use of considerable technical language relevant to the un-commonsense field of knowledge e.g. 'gold bullion', 'a series of chemical treatment(s)', 'gold particles', 'an electric current in steel wool', to mention a few;
- some skill in introducing several technical terms in ways that reveal the terms by reference to their meanings, where these are expressed in less technical or more commonsense ways. In the following examples, the technical term is italicised, and in each case it is in fact a relational process (i.e. a 'being' or sometimes a 'naming' process), either realised in 'is' or in 'called' that helps introduce the technical term:

  i   The first stage [[that the ore goes through]] is *primary crushing* . . .
  ii to form a thick mud [[called *slurry*]].
  iii Air is blown in and the slurry and chemicals are mixed together under high temperature in a process [[known as *gold leaching*]];

- the series of conjunctive relations, more varied in character than in the simple additive manner that was a feature of Text 1 above, regarding the class visit. Their effect is to build a series of interconnecting steps in the processes described, suggesting a fairly complex series of events, whose sequence and consequential effects are important;
- the very authoritative role taken up by the writer towards the reader, marked in the absence of reference to self (or indeed to any other human agent), and the consistent use of the third person throughout the text.

Before I leave discussion of Text 4, I want to draw attention to some other aspects of the linguistic resources deployed by the young writer, showing evidence of developing maturity in control of written language. The two resources are those of nominal group and circumstance, both of which I shall briefly explain first. The term 'nominal group' refers to any word or group of words that names. A pronoun such as 'he' or 'she' is a nominal group, and so is a noun such as 'gold' or 'ore'. Most commonly, however, a nominal group consists of more than one word, as in 'the small bits of ore' or 'the heavier particles of gold'. In fact, the wonderful resource that is the nominal group is capable of being expanded to 'pack in' a great deal of important information. The young writer of Text 4 very successfully uses this resource, as in the two examples just cited, as well as in for example: 'an electric current in steel wool', or 'a whole new way [[to process ore]]'. If we compare the uses of nominal group with those found in the texts by younger writers, we can see how much simpler are theirs. Consider these instances in Text 1 by a much younger writer, for example: 'we', 'a koala', 'dead foxes', 'the mountain'.

To turn to the notion of circumstance, this is a term which is used when considering processes, which have already been briefly introduced. Often, a process involves an accompanying circumstance, realised either in an adverbial group or in a prepositional phrase. Here are some examples from Text 4:

the ore is blasted *from the mine*
in the slurry the heavier particles of gold sink *to the bottom*
the slurry passes *through a series of chemical treatments*
the slurry is pumped *into a series of 12 tanks*
the carbon with gold is screened *out of the tank*
and washed *with cynanide at high temperatures.*

Again, if we compare the uses of circumstances in Text 4 with examples from Text 1, we can gauge something of the journey the young writer needs to take in learning to deploy language to create meanings, including the un-commonsense meanings of the knowledge of school learning. Thus in Text 1, we find the following instances of circumstances, all of them filling an important role, but all reasonably simple, while in some other clauses there are no circumstances at all:

we went *to Anakie Gorge*
we walked *down the path*
we climbed *up the mountain.*

Text 4 makes more frequent use of circumstances than does Text 1, and their collective effect is to build a great deal of important experiential information.

Nominal group and circumstance are two important resources for building experience and information, and always exploited to the full by successful writers. As students enter the secondary school, they often don't use these resources well, instead producing language marked by some of the simplicity of the much younger child. Developing maturity in writing will involve among other matters, learning to exploit such language resources, though there are of course other features of written language for the older writer which we will now consider.

Changing features of writing with the entry to secondary schooling

Above, I noted that the writers of texts such as Texts 1, 2 or 3 tended to create their texts by producing a series of clauses, each of which constructed a particular event, and that these events were then overtly linked through conjunctive relations. The pattern is very similar in Text 4 as well, despite its greater complexity in other ways, as we have seen. The tendency to build experience in this way represents a congruent way to build meaning. That is to say, one clause is used for one event, where the event is realised essentially in a process with accompanying participants and sometimes accompanying circumstances, as in:

From Text 1

On Wednesday	we	went	to Anakie Gorge
Circumstance	Participant	Process	Circumstance

From Text 2

put	water	in the frying pan
Process	Participant	Circumstance

From Text 3

she	put	the flower	in the liquid nitrogen
Participant	Process	Participant	Circumstance

From Text 4

the small bits of ore	are mixed	with water
Participant	Process	Circumstance

The tendency of young writers is to write series of such congruent clauses. But the tendency of much 'true written language' of the kind found in a great deal of adult life is to rearrange the grammar of independent clauses, compressing them in ways that produce incongruent realisations of the meanings involved. The process by which independent, congruent clauses are taken and rearranged is known as that of grammatical metaphor (Halliday, 1994). It compares with lexical metaphor, which is probably more familiar to most readers of this chapter. Examples of lexical metaphors occur when, for example, the poet says of the moon that it is a 'ghostly galleon tossed upon cloudy seas', or more familiarly in speech when we say of someone that 'he is a silly ass'. We sometimes forget in fact, how ubiquitous is the use of lexical metaphor as in commonplace expressions like saying that someone 'is long in the tooth', or advising someone 'to keep his head'. In such cases, we use a term to identify some action or entity that is not literally true. We do this to create a particular effect, perhaps to reinforce the point being made, or to produce a particularly powerful image for the listener or reader. The effect is to create a meaning by incongruent means.

Grammatical metaphor, as already suggested, is so called because the usual grammatical expression of the idea or experience is rearranged to express it, drawing on the grammatical resources in different ways. It is control of grammatical metaphor that is in particular important as students move into secondary education, and into the need increasingly to construct un-commonsense knowledge of many kinds. Successful emergence of grammatical metaphor and hence control of 'true written language' is a feature of late childhood and adolescence.

Let me illustrate the point by reference to a sentence I have taken from a publication giving advice on exercise (Guide to Exercise, Heart Foundation, 1982: 48): 'The possibility of runners [[being affected by heat stress]] is a major problem [[confronting fun runners]].'

This consists of one clause, with two down-ranked or embedded clauses within it, marked with the brackets [[ ]]. It is a very familiar instance of written English. If we convert the sentence to a version closer to the way it might be said in speech, we produce a more congruent version, in which I have marked in bold the conjunctive relations:

If people run
they get hot
and this can stress them
so this makes it hard [[to organise a fun run]].

Note what happens in the process of turning this to speech:

- the one clause of writing has become four clauses in speech;
- conjunctive relations between clauses in the speech build a sense of the logical relationships between the messages of the clauses;

- the spoken version says 'if people run /they get hot /and this can stress them'. Three verbal groups realising three processes are involved here: 'run', 'get' and 'can stress'. These three clauses, their processes and their relatedness are dealt with quite differently in the grammar of writing, where they are captured in a nominal group which involves one embedded clause: 'the possibility of runners [[being affected by heat stress]]'. In fact, the processes of speech and the logical relationships between clauses are transformed by creating two nominal groups 'the possibility of runners' and 'heat stress'. At the same time, the conjunctive relations are buried;
- an effect of all these grammatical changes is that the only process present in the clause is 'is'. This is an instance of a relational process, creating a relationship between two entities. Once you create two things or entities which you name through nominal groups, you can then build a connection between them through a relational process: 'The possibility of runners [[being affected by heat stress]] *is* a major problem [[confronting fun runners]].'

And now note what has happened to the part of the clause which reads 'is a major problem [[confronting fun runners]]'. In speech there is the use of a conjunction 'so' and another clause: 'so this makes it hard [[to organise a fun run]]'.

Overall, the one clause of the written version is very much denser than the four clauses of speech. That is because it is the tendency of writing to 'pack in' or compress information by use of nominal group, while it is the tendency of speech to offer information in a string of interconnected clauses, where there are many more grammatical items in use, including the conjunctions, articles, prepositions, pronouns and so on.

If at this point we look back and review the texts so far examined in this chapter, we can see that they have all tended to produce series of clauses that offered congruent realisations of their information. This tendency is particularly marked for example, in Texts 1, 2 and 3. In the case of Text 4, as we saw, the text is denser than the earlier ones because of the more elaborate use of nominal groups and circumstances, and the conjunctive relations are more varied, as befits the more complex sets of logical relationships constructed between various activities. But even then, there is no use of grammatical metaphor.

It should be noted that the extent to which a text uses grammatical metaphor is in part a condition of the field of knowledge or experience being constructed. Fields vary, though we can say that many of those constructed in the school subjects of the secondary level will use grammatical metaphor to make their meanings. Most of the texts used in this chapter have been chosen from scientific fields, where un-commonsense knowledge is an issue, though this was not of course the point in the instance of Text 1, about a class visit.

Writing in the secondary school

Text 5 was written by a student in Year 8 aged about fourteen. It is an instance of a report genre about arthritis. It is succesful for several reasons, not least that it does make effective use of grammatical metaphor in achieving control of the un-commonsense. A scientific report of the kind set out here has two elements, Classification and Description, and they are labelled. As in the case of the other texts I have examined, I have set it out clause by clause. As in earlier instances, embedded clauses are shown. Where something occurs in rounded brackets ( ), this identifies elliptical elements in the student's text.

Text 5 Arthritis

General classification
Arthritis is a disease [[which affects the joints of the body]], due to a lack of lubrication in the joints.
This causes friction
and (it causes) the bones to rub together.
The word arthritis means: inflammations [[afflicting the joints]].

Description: causes
Many of the causes of arthritis are unknown.
Some cases have been known to result from bacterial diseases like syphilis and gonorrhea or viral infections like German measles and hepatitis.
They often can lead to pains in the joints.
Injuries, particularly sport injuries, can cause arthritis to develop in later life.

Description: symptoms
Arthritis affects people of all ages.
It can cause swelling, stiffness, soreness and sharp pains in the joints, limiting mobility and movement in the affected areas.
The area around the joint may be red
and (it may) feel warm,
creating discomfort.

Description: treatment
Unfortunately, so far no complete cure is known for arthritis.
Doctors may recommend aspirin and other anti-inflammatory drugs to help relieve pain and stiffness.

Antibiotics [[to drain pus from affected joints]] may also be beneficial
for cases [[resulting from bacterial infections.]]
Injections of gold salts have proved helpful in some cases.
A long list of other drugs are questionable.
Exercises or physiotherapy may also give the sufferers relief
and (they may) help to keep the joints mobile.

Description: state of knowledge
Even though signs of arthritis have been found in dinosaur fossils,
very little is known about the disease.
But during recent times, as the awareness of the disease has grown,
more research and studies are being carried out.

(From McNamara et al., 1987: 18)

This text abounds in instances of grammatical metaphor, only some of which
I have identified in table 3.1. It is not the case that each pair in the table 'says
the same thing'. However, in each pair at least we can say that there is
a considerable similarity in the experiential information represented. Furthermore, a comparison of the two throws light on the issue of how the grammar
changes partly out of the need to shift from speech to writing and partly out
of the pressure to represent un-commonsense knowledge.

We can see that in several cases, the causal relationships between events
or items of information which are made explicit in speech are buried or at
least realised very differently. Consider the case of the opening sentence:
'Arthritis is a disease [[which affects the joints of the body]], due to a lack

Table 3.1 Grammatical metaphor

Incongruent realisation	Congruent realisation
Arthritis is a disease [[which affects the body]] due to a lack of lubrication in the joints.	Arthritis is a disease which people get in many parts of their bodies. It develops because the body joints are not lubricated properly.
This causes friction and (it causes) the bones to rub together.	The bones begin to rub together because the joints are not lubricated and they develop friction.
The word arthritis means: inflammations [[afflicting the joints]].	The word arthritis refers to what happens when the joints of the body become inflamed.
Many of the causes of arthritis are unknown.	Researchers do not know why people get arthritis.
Doctors may recommend aspirin and other anti-inflammatory drugs to help relieve pain and stiffness.	Doctors may recommend aspirin and other drugs which help control inflammation.

of lubrication in the joints.' In order to re-express the ideas here in a more congruent realisation, we have used three clauses. In addition, note that the causal connection captured in 'due to' in the written version is now made more overt with the use of the conjunction 'because' when we create the separate clause 'because the joints are not lubricated'. Finally, looking again at the written version, we can see that it has created a large nominal group 'a lack of lubrication in the joints'. The process involved in 'the joints are not lubricated' is now turned into a thing we can name as a phenomenon. This process of creating phenomena in this way is very much a part of the effect of grammatical metaphor, and it tells us something of its value. The phenomena we create become part at least of the substance of the un-commonsense learning of schooling.

We can see the same process at work for example in the instance of 'Doctors may recommend aspirin and other anti-inflammatory drugs to help relieve pain and stiffness.' The nominal group 'other inflammatory drugs' would be represented in speech as 'drugs which control inflammation'. It is important and useful to create the nominal group because it creates a thing or phenomenon important in the total pattern of building knowledge about arthritis and its treatment.

There is another sense in which the tendency of the incongruent realisations of written language is worthy of comment: it is that its effect is often to remove human agency. Consider for example 'Many of the causes of arthritis are unknown.' In the spoken or more congruent version, 'Researchers do not know why people get arthritis', two lots of humans are identified – 'researchers' and 'people'. Why might it be useful or desirable sometimes to remove humans in this way? The answer in this case is that the removal of human agency enables the writer to foreground or make prominent 'the causes of arthritis', rather than the issue of who gets it, or who researches it.

The tendency of much written language to bury human agency and hence responsibility, it should be noted, is often identified as an issue we should worry about. Where human agency is removed, it is often the case that human responsibility for events and happenings in the world is simply removed. Consider for example the following sentence which I have made up, but which draws attention to a genuine contemporary problem: 'The destruction of the rain forests in many parts of the world has caused a decline in a range of animal and plant species which hitherto lived in the forests.' The nominal group 'the destruction of the rain forests in many parts of the world' in itself obscures the fact that it is humans who destroy the forests. If the writer of the imagined text from which this sentence is drawn were not to acknowledge this, then this would be a failure to drive home the issue of whose responsibility is really involved.

Construction of nominal groups of the kind I have identified is an important aspect of the ways in which un-commonsense knowledge is constructed. The grammatical tendencies involved can be shown to be capable of being used in the construction of knowledge we may want to disagree with or to challenge. An important part of preparing students to be competent to challenge is teaching them aspects of how the grammar works to build knowledge so that they can make judgments for themselves about the values of the knowledge involved. This should be part of building the critical literacy discussed by Macken-Horarik elsewhere in this volume.

By way of bringing to a close this discussion of texts in the secondary school, I want briefly to turn to some writing in English and geography. I shall use extracts only, drawn from much longer passages of writing. I shall argue that the extracts used illustrate features of the written language students need to write and read as they grow older and move up the secondary school.

One student in Year 12 had been studying the novella by Janet Lewis called *The Wife of Martin Guerre*, and she was asked to write an argumentative text in which she discussed the characters. Her opening paragraph read:

> The strength of the novel *The Wife of Martin Guerre* is the portrayal of human qualities and values. We see in Bertrande a strong sense of right and wrong; dutifulness, we see in Bertrande and Pierre. Martin shows that he values individual freedom while Arnaud is someone who values love.

Here the student constructs qualities through use of quite elaborate nominal groups. On the one hand the qualities are in the book, as in 'the strength of the novel *The Wife of Martin Guerre*' and 'the portrayal of human qualities and values'. On the other hand, the qualities are in the characters as in 'a strong sense of right and wrong' or in 'individual freedom'.

In order to write in this manner, the writer needed to distance herself from the events of the novel to construct an argument and an interpretation, not about the details of who did what to whom, but rather about the values and moral positions that give the novel its point. To build such an argument, she had considerable recourse to the grammar of written language in order to construct statements about the moral positions of some of the characters. Herein lie some of the critical features which English students must master in order to construct abstract thought and reasoning in their writing.

Another student, this time in Year 9, and aged about sixteen years, was working on a major unit of work on World Heritage sites around the world. One of the sites he studied was Kakadu National Park, a huge tract of land in northern Australia, famous for its flora and fauna and for its sacred Aboriginal sites. In the course of a fairly substantial piece of written work in which maps and other sources were also used, one student wrote:

> The main reason for Kakadu National Park's achievement of World Heritage status is its beautiful attractions of cultural and natural significance.

Two large nominal groups here, linked by the relational process, 'is' create the one clause. As speech it would be something like the following:

> Kakadu National Park has achieved World Heritage status
> because it has many items
> that are significant culturally and naturally
> and they attract many people.

My own research in secondary schools (Christie, 1995b, 1995c, 1997), sampling students' learning in several different school subjects shows that students vary enormously in the extent to which they take up and use all the grammatical resources with which to produce written language of the kind we have been reviewing. Many students write what their teachers often recognise is language closer to speech, and they regularly receive poor grades because of this. The processes of preparing students for control of written language should commence in the primary school, and where students receive plenty of guided assistance from their teachers in studying and using the models of literate language, they will be in a strong position to enter secondary schooling. However, whatever students know at the end of primary school, it will need to be consolidated and extended at the secondary level, and here their teachers will play an important role. Development of control of many aspects of written language is a feature of late childhood and adolescence. Where teachers are aware of the particular linguistic requirements of their subjects to build their un-commonsense knowledge, they will be able to anticipate their students' needs, and to direct their learning by drawing attention to the features of literate language to be used.

Conclusion

I began this chapter with the observation that there are myths about literacy and literacy education. One myth holds that the learning of literacy is primarily a task of the early years of schooling and that thenceforth, students simply recycle the skills mastered in the first four years or so of schooling. The other myth holds that the learning of literacy is a 'natural' process, best fostered in non-interventionist ways, where the teacher's role is mainly to facilitate learning, not to direct learning of literacy. Both myths I suggested are harmful. The former is harmful because it does not acknowledge the considerable learning over years about literacy that needs to take place for students to be judged truly literate, and able to function in the contemporary world. The latter is harmful because it diminishes, sometimes even denies, the important role of the teacher in guiding and directing students' literacy. Both myths, and the models of literacy and literacy learning they represent, I suggested, suffer from an inadequate and limited understanding of language and literacy.

In this chapter I have sought to provide a sense of a better model of language and literacy by developing aspects of a functional account. While I have looked most closely at instances of written texts in this chapter, I have tried to demonstrate some of the ways in which written language differs from speech. I have suggested that the two differ grammatically and that the grammatical differences are born of the different purposes the two modes serve. Whereas speech is learned in face-to-face interaction and continues to be used that way throughout life, writing evolved to deal with experience at some remove, and it is for that purpose that it continues to be used. Thus, the grammatical features of writing reflect the fact that it creates information for the audience that is removed in terms of space and time. It is the distancing effect this generates which causes the grammatical changes as language moves from speech to writing.

Children's first attempts at writing necessarily draw upon the grammatical features of language most readily available to them, and they thus produce early texts which show aspects of the grammatical organisation of speech. In particular their tendency is to produce sequences of independent clauses, linked by a series of conjunctive relations, where each clause offers congruent representation of the experience at issue. Moreover, early writers, while certainly using nominal groups and circumstances in their writing, have yet to learn how to exploit both fully. As students grow older, a developmental task they face is that of learning how to represent experience and knowledge by the incongruent means made available through grammatical metaphor. This allows them, among other matters, to exploit the resources of the nominal group and in other ways to build written texts marked by the density that is more characteristic of writing than of speech.

I have noted that emergence of control of written language, while it certainly commences in the primary school, is a developmental feature of late childhood and adolescence. However, it is clear that not all adolescents learn to handle written language well, often struggling to deal with the un-commonsense knowledge that is a feature of the secondary school and of its increasingly differentiated curriculum. Much conventional wisdom about literacy learning never really acknowledges the very considerable developmental process that is involved in learning literacy, nor does it acknowledge the important role of teachers in both understanding the features of writing, and in teaching students to be aware of these features, in order to become effective users of literacy themselves.

Notes

1   A useful discussion and critique of the 'natural' learning theories of Goodman and Smith will be found in Reid, 1993.
2   I heard Goodman give the paper – one of several invited keynote papers – but regrettably it did not subsequently appear in the Conference Proceedings published by the SEAMEO Regional Language Centre, and edited by M. L. Tickoo.
3   These matters are discussed in detail in Halliday, 1985.
4   Incidentally, the child is writing here of a park in the Australian bush, a few kilometres from her school.
5   The notion of a process is useful because it helps us establish the type of experience being established in language through the verbal group and its associated participants. This helps us say more about the nature of the meaning constructed than does the label 'verb'. For example, 'walked', 'smiled', 'thought', 'was' are all instances of verbs, and we can label them as such. But use of the functional grammar enables us to indicate the type of process realised in each case. Respectively, they are as follows: material (having to do with action), behavioural, mental and finally relational.

References

Berger, Peter and Luckmann, Thomas, 1966 *The Social Construction of Reality.* Middlesex, England: Penguin Books.

Bernstein, Basil, 1975 *Class, Codes and Control, Vol. 3. Towards a Theory of Educational Transmissions.* London: Routledge & Kegan Paul.

Bruner, Jerome, 1986 *Actual Minds, Possible Worlds.* Cambridge, Mass.: Harvard University Press.

Christie, F., 1989 'Curriculum genres in early childhood education: a case study in writing development.' Unpublished Ph.D. thesis, University of Sydney.

——— 1991 'Literacy in Australia' in *Annual Review of Applied Linguistics,* 12, 142–155.

——— 1995a 'Pedagogic discourse in the primary school' in *Linguistics & Education,* No 3, Vol. 7, 221–242.

——— 1995b, 'The teaching of literature in the secondary English class'. *Report 1 of a Research Study into the Pedagogic Discourse of Secondary School English.* A study funded by the Australian Research Council. University of Melbourne.

——— 1995c The teaching of story writing in the junior secondary school. *Report 2 of a Research Study into the Pedagogic Discourse of Secondary School English.* A study funded by the Australian Research Council. University of Melbourne.

——— 1996 Geography. *Report of a Research Study into the Pedagogic Discourse of Secondary School Social Sciences.* A study funded by the Australian Research Council. University of Melbourne.

——— 1997 'Curriculum genres as forms of initiation into a culture' in F. Christie and J. R. Martin (eds) *Genres and Institutions: Social Processes in the Workplace and School.* London: Cassell Academic, 134–160.

Christie, F., Devlin, B., Freebody, P., Luke, A., Martin, J., Threadgold, T. and Walton, C., 1991 *Teaching English Literacy. A Project of National Significance on the Preservice Preparation of Teachers to Teach English Literacy.* Department of Education and Training & The Centre for Studies of Language in Education, Northern Territory University, Darwin, Australia.

Derewianka, B., 1996 'Language development in the transition from childhood to adolescence: the role of grammatical metaphor.' Unpub. PhD thesis, Macquarie University, Australia.

Goodman, K.S., 1982 in K. K. Gollasch (ed.) *Language and Literacy: the Selected Writings of Kenneth S. Goodman.* London: Routledge & Kegan Paul.

Goody, J. (ed.), 1968 *Literacy in Traditional Societies.* Cambridge, Cambridge University Press.

Halliday, M. A. K., 1975 *Learning How to Mean: Explorations in the Development of Language.* London: Edward Arnold.

—— 1985 *Spoken and Written Language.* Geelong Victoria: Deakin University Press (republished by Oxford University Press, 1989).

—— 1994 *An Introduction to Functional Grammar.* London: Arnold.

Hasan, R., 1985 in M. A. K. Halliday and R. Hasan *Language, Context and Text: a Social Semiotic Perspective.* Geelong Victoria: Deakin University Press (republished by Oxford University Press, 1989).

Heart Foundation, 1982 *Guide to Exercise.* National Heart Foundation of Australia, ACT.

Leakey, R., 1994 *The Origin of Mankind.* London: Weidenfeld & Nicolson.

Luria, A. R., 1976 *Cognitive Development, Its Cultural and Social Foundations.* (ed. M. Cole) Harvard: Harvard University Press.

McNamara, J., McCoughlin, R. and Baker, G., 1987 *Putting Pen to Paper: A Manual for Teachers. Practical Ideas for Writing in Science and History.* Richmond, Australia: Detail Printing.

Malinowski, B., 1923 'The problem of meaning in primitive languages' in G. K. Ogden and I. A. Richards (eds) *The Meaning of Meaning: A Study of the Influence of Language upon Thought and the Science of Symbolism.* London: Routledge & Kegan Paul.

Martin, J. R., 1992a *English text. System and Structure.* Amsterdam: John Benjamins.

—— 1992b 'Genre and literacy – modelling context in educational linguistics' in *Annual Review of Applied Linguistics,* 141–174.

Matthiessen, C., 1995 *Lexicogrammatical Cartography: English Systems.* Tokyo: International Science Publishers.

Reid, J., 1993 'Reading and spoken language: the nature of the links' in R. Beard (Ed.) *Teaching Literacy, Balancing Perspectives.* London: Hodder & Stoughton, 22–34.

Rothery, J., 1984 'The development of genres – primary to junior/secondary school' in Deakin University *Children Writing Study Guide.* Geelong, Victoria: Deakin University Press, 67–114.

Sandiford, C. 1998 'Teaching Explanations to Primary School Children. The how and the why'. Unpub. M. Ed thesis.

Smith, F. (2nd edn), 1985 *Reading.* Cambridge: Cambridge University Press.

Trevarthen, Colwyn, 1987 'Sharing makes sense: intersubjectivity and the making of an infant's meaning' in R. Steele and T. Threadgold (eds) *Language Topics.*

Essays in Honour of Michael Halliday. Amsterdam: John Benjamins, Volume 1, 177–199.

Veel, R., 1992 'Engaging with scientific language: a functional approach to the language of school science' in *Australian Science Teachers Journal,* 38, 4.

Ventola, E., 1987 *The Structure of Social Interaction.* London: Pinter.

Vygotsky, L. S. 1962 *Thought and Language.* Massachusetts: MIT Press.

4

Exploring the requirements of critical school literacy

A view from two classrooms

Mary Macken-Horarik

Introduction

The term 'critical literacy' has become a popular rubric in discussions about the kind of reading and writing students should be moving towards during their schooling. But ease of use is not clarity of reference. Just what does a critical approach to texts and textual practices entail? What kinds of linguistic proficiencies does it build on and presuppose? How are these related to the more mainstream (and perhaps mundane) proficiencies privileged in examination rooms? Is the critical literacy territory open to all students whatever their diverse starting points – their social and linguistic formations?

Even if we restrict our attention within a theorisation of literacy to the mode of 'lettered representation' as I prefer to do (see also Kress, 1997: 116), there are still multiple realities to consider. Different literacy teaching regimes foreground different skills and these have both interpretive and productive dimensions. All of the following literate skills can be said to typify the reading and writing undertaken by students at different stages of schooling:

- identifying sound/letter correspondences and developing an acceptable handwriting orthography;
- recognising the 'correct' meaning of a text or text segment and producing an 'appropriate' response to this;
- questioning the dubious messages of texts and perhaps subverting or critiquing these.

Faced with this multiplicity of skills and social specificity of uses of 'lettered representation', some scholars pluralise the term and refer to 'literacies' (Gee, 1990: 153 and Wallace, 1992a: 22). Others prefer to modify the term literacy and distinguish, for example, between 'growth literacy', 'skills literacy', 'cultural heritage literacy' and 'critical social literacy' (see, Christie *et al.*, 1991 or Ball *et al.*, 1990 for similar treatments). But even within a recognition of diverse literacy practices, hierarchy reigns supreme. One kind of practice becomes normative and is seen to subsume others. This is just what has happened with critical literacy which, however it is defined, now encompasses all other, more elementary types of literacy. The ascendancy of the term 'critical literacy' is evident in the work of Fairclough (ed.), 1992; Baker and Luke (eds), 1991: Hasan, 1995, Gilbert 1993 and Lankshear, 1994 amongst others. The following is one fairly representative viewpoint:

> A critical literacy entails *not only* a rudimentary control of the linguistic and semiotic codes of written text, *but also* understandings of the ways in which literacy has shaped the organizations and values of social life and the ways in which the texts of everyday life influence one's own identity and authority. Literacy is therefore as much about ideologies, identities and values as it is about codes and skills.
>
> (Luke, 1992: 10, my italics)

No self-respecting teacher could dispute the importance of introducing his/her students not only to the codes of written texts but also to new understandings of the relationship between such codes and social ideologies, identities and values. The semiotic and conceptual territory to be covered in a critical literacy programme is almost limitless. But there *is* a price. Less well covered in the literature on critical literacy is the linguistic challenge of moving into and through such abstract and lexically dense terrain. Just learning to read the texts produced by theorists of critical social literacy, for example, entails a massive linguistic effort. This chapter is about the linguistic skills necessary to a critical literacy and the strategies used by teachers to develop them.

If we reflect on the linguistic proficiencies necessary to a critical literacy within schooling, we are also obliged to consider the relationship between critical and mainstream literacy practices. Definitions provide one starting point in a theorisation of this relationship.

Mainstream literacy assumes an ability to read and write texts necessary for effective participation in the civic and political processes of the mainstream/dominant culture and in its specialised domains of knowledge up to a general level of competence. Reading privileges the interpretation of meaning while writing the production of meaning in these domains.

Critical literacy, on the other hand, problematises the relationship between meaning making (reading and writing) and social processes. It takes readers and writers into a reflexive world through which they can learn to recognise *and* resist the reading position(s) constructed for them by any text. Via strategies like deconstruction, critique and subversion, they come to denaturalise the taken-for-granted assumptions which underlie compliant readings and to see all texts as discursive *constructs* rather than *windows* on reality – and thus open to challenge and radical renewal. Critical literacy presupposes a high level of mainstream (reproductive) literacy.

It is also possible to consider literacy – especially mainstream literacy and critical literacy practices – from an intertextual point of view. The term 'intertextuality' refers to *relations between texts* – both those which texts implicitly take for granted or explicitly allude to and those which readers bring to their reading of them. As Jay Lemke describes these relations:

> Every text, the discourse of every occasion, makes sense in part through implicit and explicit relationships of particular kinds to other texts, to the discourse of other occasions. A story may be heard as a fable in the manner of Aesop, belonging to a genre which among other features has a characteristic internal organizational structure. It may be functioning as a rejoinder to yesterday's argument to be part of a larger structure of action over time, and it may echo and develop the themes of that argument or of other storytellings with which it has no recognized structural relations. The discourse practices of a community both build systems of texts related in these ways and establish the recognised kinds of relationships there may be between texts or the discourse of different occasions.
>
> (Lemke, 1985: 275)

The intertexts of any text are all the other texts that we use to make sense of it and these will vary from reader to reader (and community to community). Our students bring into our classrooms not just experiences of 'reality' but experiences of different kinds of texts. Both vary. The reading one student makes of a text will depend partly on which other texts s/he regards as relevant to its interpretation. His or her intertextuality may or may not mesh with that valued in school learning. (See Misson in this volume, for a related discussion.)

In my own research into students' responses to narratives, I discovered that students activate different intertexts according to their interpretation of a context. Classifying the context is especially difficult, however, when the nature of the task is unclear (Macken-Horarik, 1996). In the New South Wales Reference Test, for example, literacy tasks in English are so open-ended that they facilitate misrecognition of the context (and activation of an inappropriate intertextuality).[1] Examinees may be invited to write about why they 'think a given story ends the way it does' (1986 Reference Test), to 'tell the author what they think of her story' (1990 Reference Test) or to explain 'the real meaning of the story' (1995 Reference Test). Some interpret the task as a request for a personal response, providing a feeling reaction to the story; others for a précis, providing a summative retelling of the story; and still others for an interpretive response, providing a traditional literary criticism about the story's abstract significance. In short, different examinees draw on different intertexts. Of course not all interpretive strategies (and hence intertexts) are equally valued by examiners. This is predictable. The point is that examination success has less to do with the meanings immanent 'within' a stimulus narrative than with the intertextualities examinees bring to it.

The notion of intertextuality is useful because it enables us to connect students' already developed literacy practices with the practices valued in or marginalised by schooling. Intertextuality thus faces two ways: towards the reader and his/her experiences and towards the text itself and all the other texts it implicates. Texts constrain the possible interpretations that can plausibly be made of them (and the intertexts which are relevant) but readers take these up in different ways. Intertextuality thus has both an interpretive (readerly) and a productive (writerly) dimension and we need to bring both aspects into our picture of literacy education. This is important because some relations between texts are more salient in some learning contexts than others. Knowing which intertexts are 'in play' and mediating their significance for students is a pedagogic responsibility. One made even more challenging because the language of academic learning is increasingly technical, abstract and linguistically metaphorical as the school years go by. (See Christie in this volume for some discussion of this point.)

But how do we characterise intertextuality in literacy education? For me, the notion of *register* has been a useful way of characterising the meaning potential privileged in particular situation types and that of *genre* the text types typically produced within these. In my own research I cluster registers and genres according to their function within four contextual domains which interface with school learning: the Everyday, the Applied, the Theoretical and the Reflexive domains. As table 4.1 shows, each domain is associated with a particular kind of literacy (and intertextuality).

It is specialised and critical literacy practices which are in focus in this chapter (for a more extended discussion of the contextual domains see Macken-Horarik, 1995, 1996). Drawing on the functional language model developed by Halliday, Martin, Christie and Rothery amongst others, we can represent our students' intertextualities in a linguistically principled way, interpreting these from the point of view of the *registers* (meaning potentials) they can operate within and the *genres* (text types) they know how to produce (see Christie, this volume).

Of course, no construct is adequate to all the factors that educators need to take account of in their literacy teaching. The genre-based extensions of Halliday's model of language have been overly pedagocentric, valorising teachers' perspectives on the demands and possibilities of school learning. Learners' perspectives also need to be incorporated. Nevertheless, teachers *do* bear an onerous responsibility for assisting students from poorer and non-English speaking backgrounds to gain access to specialised and critical literacy practices. Without the guidance of one who mediates the proficiencies necessary to such literacy practices, many students are stranded indefinitely within personalist and often idiosyncratic readings of contexts, without the tools for analysing and (if necessary) resisting their demands.

Table 4.1 A view of the meaning and practices privileged within four domains

Everyday	Applied	Theoretical	Reflexive
Starting points: diverse and open ended	**Gaining control of specific kinds of expertise**	**Accessing dominant forms of knowledge and semiosis**	**Negotiating social diversity and competing discourses**
I	2	3	4
Working with the contents of tacit knowledge, based on personal and communal experience	Using a specific skill or 'know how', based on acquired expertise	Assimilating and reproducing the contents of specialised knowledge, based on educational learning	Questioning the taken-for-granted understandings of specialised knowledge, based on alternative perspectives
Playing out the roles and relationships of family, kin and community networks	Taking up an apprenticeship role relevant to a particular practice	Becoming an incumbent member of a discipline	Challenging and reconstituting roles in a world of social diversity
Interacting with others, primarily through spoken language	Using spoken and written language to enable experience or activity	Producing and interpreting epistemic texts	Reconstruing meanings through different media
'personal growth literacy'	**'skills literacy'**	**specialised literacy'**	**'critical literacy'**

What are the implications of this representation of literacy? If we accept the pre-eminent importance of critical literacy, then we must construe it as a dependent phenomenon. While critical literacy should not be regarded as 'frills' or as 'an add on' (Luke *et al.*, 1996: 42), it is nevertheless *dependent* on students' prior engagement with mainstream/specialised literacy practices. The intertextualities on which such practices are founded are not separate lines of development but mutually informing and reinforcing. But within school education at any rate, I would argue that there is no way into critical literacy practices but through those of the mainstream. This is not a conservative argument in support of the preservation of the social status quo in literacy education. I prefer to think of it as a social justice argument that seeks to open up critical literacy for *all* students. It is not fair to invite our students to critique texts before they have learned to analyse them and still less fair to those who cannot yet even process their meanings.

In the classrooms which provided the case study material for the present study, teachers considered literacy in developmental terms and saw their task as one of opening up pathways into critical as well as specialised literacy practices. A perspective that views literacy as a lifelong process makes it easier to plan for and track the development of new (albeit inter-related) intertextualities which themselves can lead to changing social practices. In the remainder of this chapter I discuss classroom data which supports the proposal that there are (at least) *three requirements* of a critical literacy within schooling.

Students need to:

1 gain access to a range of *contextualisation* practices in their reading and writing;
2 develop *meta-level awareness* of texts and the practices they instantiate;
3 acquire both of the above within visible pedagogies marked by *explicit-ness*.

These are foundational requirements for a critical school literacy – a critical intertextuality. I will deal briefly with each point before exploring their classroom embodiments.

Contextualisation

Advocates of critical literacy practices emphasise relationships between textual meanings and social practices and contend that students need to learn how to analyse, and critique these relationships. Gilbert, for example, argues that 'A grasp of "critical" literacy – of what I would call the social contextualisation of language practices – necessitates a grasp of how language operates in a social sense' (Gilbert, 1993: 324). But, while Gilbert foregrounds the social dimensions of contextualisation, I would argue that contextualisation is a feature of *all* language practices – whether these are interpreted in everyday, applied, theoretical or critical terms. Halliday maintains that contextualisation is a feature of learning generally – a building up of expectancies about the demands and the potentials of any social context (Halliday in Halliday and Hasan 1985: 49).

What kinds of contextualisation are germane to critical literacy practices? How do these relate to specialised literacy practices? In English examinations, for example, students can expect to be asked to interpret literary texts such as short stories or poems. In order to deal successfully with such tasks, they need to recognise the nature of the institution from which they emanate and signal this by producing a text in an appropriate genre. In the examination context, therefore, their response needs to be aligned with the interests and agendas of those 'in charge' of the examination. A specialised contextualisation of a response task like this one will typically lead to production of a piece of traditional literary criticism rather than to a personal response.

But what would a more 'resistant' reading of an interpretive task look like? Students with a critical orientation to the occasion will recognise but may reconstrue its requirements. They may use the occasion (including the genre by which they instantiate this) to explore alternative agendas and interests and draw on relevant intertexts in unexpected ways. For instance, they may deconstruct the literary text in ways which overturn the assumptions underlying the question or take issue with the question itself. Of course, resisting the institutionally valued reading of a context is not necessarily a sensible move to make – especially in examinations. Students need to make informed decisions about which occasions warrant a critical and which ones a more mainstream reading.

A critical orientation situates any given text within alternative discourses – of which the text itself may be unconscious. Of course, a prior facility will need to be in place here: students need to be able to contextualise a text in terms which *it* makes obvious before they can be expected to reframe it in alternative terms. Recognition comes before recontextualisation. The point is to open up students to a range of contextualisation frames. Table 4.2 demonstrates which kinds of contextualisation typify specialised and critical literacy practices. Drawing on Halliday's three metafunctions, they are modelled in ideational, interpersonal and textual terms respectively. (See Christie, this volume, for some discussion of these terms.)

Meta-level awareness

Much of the theoretical literature advocating critical literacy is addressed to teachers of students with already well-developed literacy proficiencies. Its 'ideal reader' is presumed to be able to answer questions such as the following after an initial reading of a text:

1 What is the topic?
2 Who is writing to whom?
3 How is this topic being written about?

Table 4.2 Interrelating specialised and critical intertextualities

A specialized intertextuality	A critical intertextuality
Students need to:	Students can:
• recognise the contextual requirements of a task and realise this in a text of the 'appropriate genre'.	• recognise but reconstrue the contextual requirements of a communicative occasion.
• align their interests and agendas with those 'in charge' of the writing context.	• use the occasion (including the genre) to explore new interests and agendas.
• draw on institutionally relevant intertexts in the production of their response text.	• draw on relevant intertexts in new and unexpected ways as they 'play with' readerly expectations of the occasion (and the genre).

4 Why is this topic being written about?
5 What other ways of writing about the topic are there?
   [suggested by Wallace (1992b) and Lankshear (1994) following Kress (1989)]

Such questions appear simple enough to literate readers who are familiar with the field within which a text is situated. But any reader who can recognise a text's topic, identify its implied author and readership and comment on its rhetorical features is no longer a beginner. S/he already demonstrates meta-level awareness – an ability to consider text as construct.

The category of genre represents one 'way in' to this dimension of intertextuality – a way which teachers have found particularly valuable. In the literacy interventions which I have had most to do with, genre has raised teachers' consciousness about a wide range of factual and non-factual text types important for school learning and community participation (see Martin, 1993 for a review of genre in different educational sites). Primary and secondary teachers who trialled the approach reported that it gave them 'something to shoot for' in classroom work. It enabled them to orient students to the overall structure of prototypical text types and their functional elements (or stages). As the case study data makes clear, this is helpful when it comes to writing, as all students become 'party to literacy requirements' and share in a metalanguage which spells out clearly what their texts need to include.

Like texts themselves, meta-level awareness can also be metafunctionally differentiated. Interpretations may focus on experiential meaning – not just the topic of a text but the treatment it gives to this. They may focus on interpersonal meaning and draw inferences about the agenda(s) of a writer and his/her 'designs' on the reader. Or, they may focus on textual meanings and analyse the compositional or rhetorical features of texts. What is important is that students get access to resources which enable them to distance themselves from texts (see them from 'above or round about'). As will be seen, 'getting meta' is crucial to both specialised and critical intertextualities.

Explicitness

Students who have learned to contextualise texts in alternative ways and to apply meta-level awareness to their interpretation/production of them have drawn in resourceful ways on the pedagogies employed by their teachers (amongst other mentors). Many students will not gain access to these resources without a visible pedagogy – one whose principles are accessible to scrutiny. As case study data attests, explicitness is an important component of a visible pedagogy. And this extends not only to knowledge about registers and genres but to knowledge about the relative value these are accorded in different institutions. As I noted earlier, teachers play a crucial role in helping students discern which intertexts are relevant in which contexts. Reading contexts is just as important as reading texts.

What kind of teaching strategies facilitate explicitness? The Sydney teachers who were first introduced to the functional language model during inservices run by the Disadvantaged Schools Program in the late 1980s and early 1990s used strategies such as modelling or joint negotiation (see, for example, Callaghan and Rothery, 1988 for a description of the curriculum genre later known as the 'teaching/learning cycle'). These proved useful because they enabled learners to make connections between different social purposes and different text types. The structure and features of these text types could be explicated through focussed reading of model texts or through joint construction of a class text. Teachers were thus able to support students' efforts with a new genre by pointing up its distinctive features or by co-creating a possible text with them. Learners were thus 'in on the act' from the outset, sharing understandings not only about the structure and language of genres but their relation to different purposes and contexts.

As case study data shows, teachers' input into work on a new genre is typically exhaustive, especially with students whose intertextualities are not aligned closely with those privileged within school learning. This kind of input demands more than a simple induction into the generic structure of key genres. It calls for reading and writing programmes which immerse students in texts intertextually relevant to different learning contexts. This kind of teaching, I believe, offers students opportunities for discourse appropriation rather than simple discourse reproduction (however, see Cranny-Francis and Martin 1995; Luke 1995 and Hasan 1995 for useful discussions of the issues arising from genre-based pedagogies).

Each of the above points – gaining access to a range of contextualisation practices, development of meta-level awareness and explicitness in pedagogic practices – can now be exemplified.

During the period 1990–1992, I worked in intensive blocks of time with Margaret Watts in science and Bill Simon in English as they applied the functional language model to teaching literacy in their subject. The data featured here was collected from different schools over the course of one unit of work in English (six weeks) and Science (ten weeks). Like others working in disadvantaged schools, Margaret and Bill undertook inservices about new approaches to teaching literacy for pragmatic reasons. They wanted access to a metalanguage which would help them to improve the literacy proficiencies of particularly non-English speaking background students. However, once they had discovered the utilitarian value of genre for teaching students about basic structure of text types such as narrative and exposition in English and report, explanation and procedure in science, both teachers expressed an interest in extending the model in the direction of greater usefulness, especially with respect to critical literacy.[2]

The biology unit with Year 10

Margaret Watt's biology unit focussed on writing explanations within the study of reproduction technologies. Margaret planned to review earlier work on elementary principles of human reproduction, then move on to cover new ground on inheritance and the use of technologies such as in-vitro fertilisation (often referred to as IVF). This unit was concerned to explore the relationship between science and society and the explanation genre was vital to both interests. The diverse perspectives Margaret wanted to explore are reflected in her learning objectives.

At the end of this unit of work, students should be able to:

- Use the explanation genre effectively.
- Explain the processes of sexual reproduction in humans, In-Vitro Fertilisation, Genetic Engineering and Inheritance (both dominant and recessive).
- List and describe the technologies for intervening in or altering the outcomes of human reproduction.
- Discuss the ethical and social issues arising out of new reproduction technologies.
- Read and discuss various issues treated in a number of articles (newspapers, scientific journals, textbooks) and in different media (both print and television).

What steps, then, did she take to move her students from their current understandings to those privileged within the discipline?

Students' commonsense knowledge of human reproduction was mediated by personal experiences in their everyday lives and certainly would not have been uniform. Only some of the class had done some earlier work on reproduction, so Margaret began by reviewing this and establishing a common knowledge base for all the class. A complete account of the work done in this initial period is beyond the scope of the chapter. However, it is possible to comment briefly on the direction which classroom work took and its relation to some of the reading and writing students did as a result. In early work they labelled diagrams of the male and female reproductive organs, assigning technical names to body parts. Diagrams of the kind used represent the familiar world of sexual organs from a biological perspective. They transform the body into a site of reproductive organs and processes. The technical terms introduced in the diagrams could be reused in explanatory schemas such as science Text 1.

Science Text 1: The female reproductive system

When a girl is born, she has many undeveloped eggs in each _____.
These eggs are called _____. Once puberty begins, these eggs will be
released and travel down the _____ _____ to the thick, muscular
_____ where a baby can develop. The large tube leading from the
uterus is called the _____. The folds of skin around the entrance to
the vagina are called _____.

Somewhere between the ages of 10 and 15, some of the eggs in a
girl's ovaries develop. One egg is released from an ovary about every
____ weeks. This tiny egg moves along the oviduct (also called a
_____) towards the _____. While the egg is developed, released, and
moving down the tube, a thick _____ continues to develop in the
uterus.

If the egg is not fertilised, part of the lining, together with liquid and
some blood, comes out through the _____ during _____. This 'period'
usually lasts ___ days. The whole cycle usually takes about ___ days
and is controlled by _____.

Once students were able to identify organs like ovaries, fallopian tubes and
the uterus on the diagram, they could assign them to their right place in
cloze passages about menstruation, fertilisation, pregnancy and birth. Each
part of the human reproductive system now became functionally linked to
others in a dynamic chain of biological processes. This technical recontextualisation of the body thus took female students beyond a localised
experience of sexual organs and a monthly period into *biological* representations of menstruation. This was, in effect, a new intertextuality,
enabling learners to 'technicalise' a familiar area of experience. In terms of
table 4.1, students were being inducted into an 'applied intertextuality' –
in which language is close to observable phenomena and readers rely
heavily on extra-linguistic cues to help them decode texts.

The class wrote an initial explanation about how the sex of a child is
determined and then worked on the different stages of 'egg development'
in gestation. The students also drew up a table summarising the events
from 0 hours to twelve days after conception. Work on fertilisation was
important if they were to understand the timing of the IVF procedure,
which they turned to next. At this point, Margaret showed a video
programme on IVF to the class and asked them to write a short account of
the process based on the notes they made during this programme.
Foundational work of this kind was crucial – especially for members of the
class who were not present for work done in previous years. Margaret
supported such students by orally rehearsing new terms and activity

sequences with them before they began work on diagrams, flow charts and cloze exercises. Such students were not expected to work independently at this stage and typically completed their exercises in small groups drawing on the expertise of the teacher or other students.

It was at this point that Margaret stopped work on 'science' and focussed on an important text type through which scientific knowledge is constructed: the explanation (the terms 'genre' and 'text type' were used interchangeably). In an important sense, language itself became the field of study. How did she introduce students to this genre?

Students' first efforts at explaining how the sex of a child is determined had provided her with information about their starting points *vis à vis* the genre and what areas of their written work needed attention. Because they had had no guidance about the structure and nature of scientific genres, Margaret introduced the class first to key written genres like explanations, reports, procedures, expositions and discussions. The links between genre and the notion of social purpose were explained and students worked in groups matching examples of each genre with its social purpose and its text type. The class discussed differences between these genres. Then Margaret narrowed the focus to a discussion of two genres – explanation and report – and students explored contrasts between these. Some observed that the explanation featured causal connectors and was more about 'things in action' (processes) than 'things in place' (taxonomies), as in reports. The class spent at least one week looking at explanations before beginning to write their own.

Margaret structured the students' first 'official' explanation as a 'way in' to work on IVF. She modelled the target text on an overhead projector – breaking it down into its component stages and listing the technical verbs necessary to explain the IVF sequence. Processes like 'fertilise', 'block', 'transfer' and ovulate', were crucial to reconstruction of this procedure and she situated them in the outline using the following framework:

Task: Explain the In-Vitro Fertilisation Process

1 Define IVF
2 Outline situation: people who need IVF
(e.g. fertilise, block, transfer, travel)
3 Explain procedure
(e.g. ovulate, masturbate, removal, transfer, place, mix)
. . . Embryo Implantation
. . . Return of embryo (e.g. insert, implant remove, wait)

Margaret's board notes

Students drafted explanations in groups, then wrote their final drafts independently following editing of their work by Margaret. Science Text 2 demonstrates how one student – Beth – was able to integrate her knowledge of the procedure with new awareness of the structure of the genre.

Science Text 2: Explanation of how IVF works

IVF involves fertilisation of the egg outside the woman's body.

Participants are infertile couples, where either the woman has a damaged fallopian tube or the man has a low sperm count, wishing to have a child.

When the man produces the sperm, it is mixed with the egg that has been removed from the woman's ovary. Fertilisation occurs on the petri dish.

Two or three days later, the embryo is placed into the uterus by way of a long thin tube. At about this time the egg would be arriving from the fallopian tube in normal circumstances.

Four or five days after the insertion of the egg, it should start to attach itself to the wall of the womb. If this occurs successfully, the embryo embeds and continues to develop.

Beth

As can be observed, students' first explanations were highly reproductive (in two senses). They were explicitly scaffolded through the board notes and amounted to little more than a 'filling out' of their teacher's schema. Margaret was openly interventionist in her modelling of the genre. In her own words:

> I explicitly model the language requirements of the genre. I show students and tell them how to do it – step one, two, three, etcetera. I show the connectors, the processes – I am *really* down at language level. But later they have the means for dealing with the language on their own. They can deconstruct texts themselves even in exams – the language functions are there even in the short answer questions.
>
> (Margaret Watts, personal communication)

Following this work on the explanation, students moved on to more demanding work on inheritance. In particular, they investigated Mendelian inheritance – including recessive and dominant genes and how these influence nose shape, and eye and hair colour amongst other characteristics. If we consider the three explanations they produced after being introduced to the genre, we can see how each subsequent writing task builds on knowledge already established in prior lessons:

Task 1 Explain the process of In-Vitro Fertilisation

Task 2 Write a letter to a couple who have embarked on the IVF programme. Explain to the couple why it is that their child may be very different from them.

Task 3 Explain how the material of inheritance may be changed.

As can be seen, the explanations became more complex, moving from more material sequences about IVF to more theoretical ones about changing the material of inheritance. Students were thus introduced to a chain of increasingly complex intertexts which built on each other with respect to field knowledge. Furthermore, this complexity was more than just ideational. Explaining the process of inheritance to IVF parents demanded not only technical knowledge of IVF and of inheritance but an ability to reformulate this in terms understandable to a lay audience. This kind of writing puts pressure on students' interpersonal resources. It requires an ability to integrate two perspectives on a technical process – those of the scientist with his or her specialised knowledge of inheritance and those of the layperson with more or less commonsense understandings of how children come to be like their parents.

Science Text 3 demonstrates one student's attempt to negotiate these competing demands. Although Rodney handles this difficult task well, he combines the two registers (everyday and theoretical) somewhat awkwardly.

Science Text 3

Follows is an explanation of why an offspring from a couple in the IVF programme receiving either sperm, ovum or both would not have a baby that looks like the birth mother and/or father.

When an ova is produced in the woman's ovary, it is given 23 of the mother's 46 chromosomes. These chromosomes make up the nucleus of the cells in the ova. Lying along each chromosome are 1,000 or more genes. Contained in these genes is DNA or the genetic information that determines such characteristics as eye colour, nose shape, height and many other characteristics. This process also occurs in the father's sperm. He too passes on his genetics to the unborn zygote. Thus when fertilisation occurs, the baby's characteristics are decided, the dominant genes develop while the recessive genes lay dormant to be passed on in the next generation. This therefore explains the fact that it doesn't matter who the embryo implants and grows in, but what really matters is who produced the ova and sperm in the beginning.

Rodney

New reproduction technologies such as IVF make it possible to separate the processes of fertilisation (affecting heredity) and gestation (affecting carriage of the baby to birth). Rodney has been able to explain the influence of this disjunction between 'who produced the ova and sperm in the beginning' and 'who the embryo implants and grows in' quite adequately, despite his rather inappropriate reference to the growing baby as an 'unborn zygote'.

Explanations such as this provide evidence of a student's learning. In this unit, Margaret assessed students primarily through their writing:

> The language they're using shows me what they're learning. You can't write an explanation of a process unless you *really* understand it. Writing an explanation forces you to come to an understanding of how one event is logically related to others.
>
> (Margaret Watts, personal communication)

While the complexity increased in the course of the unit, Margaret did not attempt to 'do it all' at the same time. In fact, she asked students to deal with one challenge at a time. Work on genre temporarily supplanted work on field knowledge but once students had control of the structure and features of the explanation, they drew on this more implicitly in later work. In earlier work, however, they needed to see language as a field of study just as important as science itself.

How did students draw on their field knowledge to dialogue with other discourses and to question different constructions of knowledge? Students read around the field intensively over the whole unit of work. This rich inter-textual territory included text book material, newspaper and magazine articles on issues such as IVF, DNA fingerprinting, gene splicing, cloning and genetic engineering in general. The class noticeboard was given over to news-paper articles collected by students and sometimes the early part of the lesson was spent on the latest acquisitions and the issues they raised. The class also watched and wrote up videos on sex determination, IVF and surrogacy – all of which treated specialised knowledge as problematic in one way or another.

While Margaret did not wait until the end of the unit to move into more reflexive work on these issues, there was a rhythm to her interventions. She only asked her students to consider an issue when they knew enough about the 'science' behind it. For example, students talked about who owned the child in the Donor Gamete Program: the donor of the gamete or the woman whose uterus grows the baby? But their ability to participate effectively in discussions was dependent on their understanding of how the programme worked and the roles different people play in it. In later lessons, the class talked extensively about the advantages and disad-vantages of advances in genetic engineering – taking up such questions as the dangers to future generations of errors in genetic experiments or the possibility of new forms of 'germ warfare' falling into the wrong hands.

Nor did they leave the media out of the picture. One of the students' final tasks involved answering questions related to news reports about advances in genetic technology. Students were presented with newspaper articles about 'cures' based on these advances. The first of these articles is reprinted below:

Doctors find cure for cystic fibrosis

from Margaret Harris in London

Doctors in London and Berlin have developed a test which can eliminate cystic fibrosis

The test – which relies on genetic analysis of a single cell removed from an eight-celled embryo conceived using in-vitro fertilisation techniques – will be used to allow women known to be carrying genetic diseases to have normal children.

Careful removal of one cell at this early stage should not damage the embryo. If, when the cell has been analysed, the embryo is proven to be free of the cystic fibrosis gene, the embryo can be implanted in its mother's womb and develop into a normal healthy baby.

Writing up their work in the *British Medical Journal*, the London team from Hammersmith Hospital said they were ready to use these techniques to eliminate a wide range of genetic diseases. Easiest to identify are the sex-linked diseases carried on the 'X' chromosome because only males are seriously affected.

Embryos of mothers known to carry the hemophilia gene can have their cells examined to determine whether or not they are males. Only female embryos will be implanted in mothers known to be carrying the hemophilia gene.

Although the research team at Hammersmith Hospital say their techniques will eliminate serious genetic diseases like cystic fibrosis, campaigners opposed to genetic research, genetic manipulation and abortion say their work should be stopped.

Margaret asked the class to apply their scientific knowledge to a reading of texts like these. One of her questions was: 'Are these cures? If not, what are these articles describing?' Science Text 4 is one student's response to this question:

Science Text 4

The so called cures that doctors have come up with for cystic fibrosis are nothing more than prevention of the inherited disease being developed in an embryo.

Rodney

Notice Rodney's use of 'so called' to modify the nominal 'cures'. This device is an index of his ability to semioticise his distance from the verbal representations of others. An important step on the way to becoming critically literate is to see others' texts as constructs which can be resisted and, in this case, directly challenged. He resists the newspaper text's attempt to position him as an uncritical consumer of news about 'scientific cures' and deconstructs this using the knowledge he has acquired about reproduction technologies. He is moving into a critical intertextuality via the specialised intertextuality he has developed through his earlier work.

By the end of the unit, the field of reproduction technology became more and more 'fraught' and it is no accident that students were forced to make greater use of discussion and critique in both spoken and written modes. Their intertextualities were becoming more complex, like the field itself. They were now interpreting such technologies from the point of view of everyday issues for consumers (the cost of IVF), from the point of view of the discipline itself (how genetic engineering builds on knowledge about inheritance) and from more reflexive points of view (the ethics of freezing embryos for research purposes) and so on.

If all learning involves contextualisation of some kind, in Margaret Watt's biology classroom, students gained access to (at least) three contextual frames by which to interpret developments in reproduction technologies. As table 4.1 outlines these frames, learners now contextualised these technologies in applied, theoretical and reflexive terms. The 'social contextualisation' which Gilbert envisages for development of a critical literacy may be better represented as only one point on a continuum which involves different kinds of contextualisation (and intertextualities). These students first had to deal with the intertextuality privileged in the discipline itself before they could engage effectively (as incumbent scientists) with those which challenge its criterial assumptions or those who market its advances (as in news media). The work done in Margaret's classroom during this ten weeks reveals something of the complexity involved in developing these intertextualities and their associated literacy practices.

The romance unit with Year 9

The importance of the teacher's mediating role in building up alternative contextual frames for analysing texts is also well exemplified in Bill Simon's English classroom. Most of his Year 9 class came from diverse non-English speaking backgrounds (including Greek, Arabic, Vietnamese, Polynesian and Serbian) with only two members from Anglo-Australian backgrounds. As will be seen, this combination of backgrounds and different beliefs about women's roles made for interesting class discussions about the place of romance in life partnerships. In this unit, Bill planned to introduce students to the romance genre in fictional and filmic media.

The goals of his unit were as follows:

- To explore the characteristics of the romance genre in two media – fiction and film.
- To investigate the extent to which the film makers exploit the possibilities of the genre to suit different audiences – school age and older (e.g. in what ways is *Pretty in Pink* a kid pic? What views of women are represented in *Pretty Woman?*)
- To write, recreate and critique different texts in the romance genre.

Bill's goals involved both interpretation and production of romance narratives. First, students would study the features of the genre in stories from *Head Over Heels: Creative Writing through Romantic Fiction* (McRobbie, 1990). Second, they would write their own romance. Finally, this initial work would strengthen their abilities to deconstruct and critique the messages of romantic films such as *Pretty Woman*.

Although this case study focusses on the romance genre, most members of the class had already done some work on narrative. In Year 8 they had analysed the structure of short stories using the Labovian stages of Orientation, Complication, Evaluation and Reorientation. This simple schema was one of the intertextual frames taken for granted in early work here. Now students were introduced to a 'romance inflection' on this. Stereotypical romance narratives have four major stages – Meeting, Finding, Losing and Ending and this schema could be usefully applied to all the stories in the McRobbie anthology. Following extensive reading of these stories, students were asked to develop their own romance narratives using stimulus titles such as 'Love on the dole', 'Revenge is sweet' or 'Pride, progress and passion'. Student pairs built up their plot summaries using formulas like the one in figure 4.1. Flow charts like this one poke good-natured fun at the predictability of plot lines in the romance genre but they also serve to orient readers to its global structure – its semiotic 'constructedness'. By such means, students learn about the kinds of experience made possible in the romance: prototypically, a heroine's search for psycho-sexual fulfilment through rescue by a dominant/male hero.

English Text 1 is an excerpt from a narrative written by two students using one of the stimulus titles and demonstrates how these writers were able to use the formula to structure a narrative that, in its passionate 'frisson', rivals the ubiquitous Mills and Boon novel. The original text itself is too long to reproduce in this context, so sections relevant to the four stages (Meeting, Finding, Losing, Ending) are displayed as follows:

English Text 1: Pride, progress and passion

Meeting   He turned to face the most entrancing and tender woman that his dazzling yellow-green eyes had ever encountered. Her beauty bewitched him and the dress she displayed, revealed the figure that every woman dreamed to possess. As Aurora reached the foot of the staircase, her enchanting, innocent eyes gazed up at him behind long, black lashes. She slowly yet elegantly advanced towards him.

Finding   He kissed her lightly on the hand, then pulled her hand so it was caressing his cheek. 'Such soft, delicate hands.' Kenneth realised what he was doing and instantly let her hand drop beside her. Aurora was blushing. If it weren't for the rouge, he would have noticed. She smiled at him and he grinned back.

Losing   Tonight when everything was so quiet, she could close her eyes and imagine she was back in the rural stillness of her 'home' and that life was unchanging, unchanging. But she knew life would never be the same.

'Oh Eleanor' she sobbed.

Ending   Aurora heard the door click and she hastily raised her head and dashed her hand across her wet eyes. She rose and saw it was Kenneth. Aurora was silent, embarrassed. His eyes flickered with amusement. 'What luck.' he said softly, 'to find you alone.' Something in his voice made her heart beat pleasantly faster and she felt her face flush. Taking her hand, he turned it over and pressed his lips into the palm. Something vital, electric leaped from him to her at the touch of his warm mouth, something that caressed her whole body thrillingly. His lips travelled to her wrist and she knew he must feel the leap of her pulse as her heart quickened and she tried to draw back her hand.

'I love you! Your courage and your stubbornness and your fire and your utter ruthlessness. How much do I love you? So much to ask you to become my wife . . . ' They fell silent and looked at each other.

This was the beginning . . . 'Yesterday is not ours to recover, but tomorrow is ours to win or lose.'

(Stephanie and Angelique)

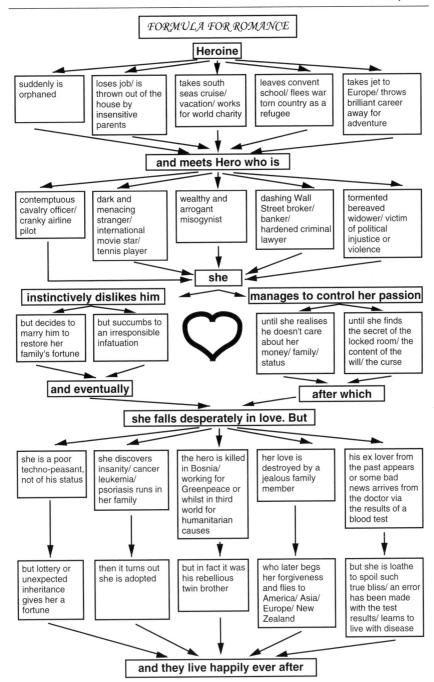

Figure 4.1 Bill's romance formula

Student writers like Stephanie and Angelique do not produce texts like 'Passion, pride and progress' by accident. Their earlier analytical work on narrative – examining romances using the given formula, developing character profiles and plot summaries for a number of these – gave them a handle on the genre when the time came to write their own romance. Furthermore, being formulaic was something to be cultivated rather than avoided in this task. Gaining control of this genre meant learning about how it 'packages experience'. Or, as Bill reminded the students: 'Things turn out the way they do *because* of the formula.'

It was this kind of meta-level awareness that enabled them to exploit its potential in their writing. In English Text 1, for example, this awareness seems to animate not only the macro-structure of their story but more micro aspects of its experiential world as well. The writers conjoin heavily descriptive nominal groups such as '*the most entrancing and tender woman* that *his dazzling yellow-green eyes* had ever encountered' or '*her enchanting, innocent eyes* gazed up at him behind *long black lashes*' with 'juicy' processes, creating an overheated world of desire and unfulfilled longing: 'Her beauty *bewitched* him'; 'Her eyes *gazed* up at him'; 'He *kissed* her lightly on the hand and then *pulled* her hand so that it was *caressing* his cheek' and so on.

How did such writers get to this point? Through a combination of Bill's explicit modelling of the formula and through wide reading of generically similar texts (both inside and outside the classroom). These explicit and implicit ways of learning appeared to encourage an emulative intertextuality in students – one which enabled them to mimic the semiotic strategies of published romance writers. In fact, learning to do in classroom writing what 'real authors' do is part of the curriculum in English in the junior secondary years (whether hidden from view or made more visible, as in this classroom). At any rate, by about week three of this unit, Bill's students had 'imbibed' enough of the meaning potential of romance to write really convincing (albeit occasionally 'overwritten') examples of the genre. Their texts were collected, printed, and distributed to other classes in the school.

After this the class turned its attention to film romances – a shift of medium if not of genre. Students applied the same metalanguage to analysis of two Hollywood romances *Pretty Woman* and *Pretty in Pink*. English Text 2 comes from notes on the plot structure of *Pretty in Pink*, written by a class group led by Filippa.

English Text 2: Plot structure analysis

Meeting   Andie meets Blane. She is rude to Blane and he seeks her out in the record store where she works.

Finding   Andie wants to go out with Blane but is ashamed of her poverty and whether he will reject her because of it. She agrees to go on a date with him but not to be picked up from her house.

Losing   Blane's best friend is rejected by Andie for his aggressive advances and then humiliates Blane for going out with Andie – a girl from the 'wrong side of the tracks'. Blane decides not to go to the Prom with Andie.

Ending   Andie decides to go to the Prom anyway 'just to let him (Blane) know that he didn't break me'. Ducky (Andie's friend) picks her up and takes her in. Blane arrives and apologises to Andie for his behaviour. Ducky lets her go and Blane and Andie kiss.

(Filippa's group)

The class also analysed the features of *Pretty in Pink* that make it a good example of a 'kid pic'. These included elements like its stages, its setting, types of character and its 'reality' (e.g. showing that 'love conquers all differences'). Students were asked to take one or two of the elements of kid pix, apply them to the movie and then report to the rest of the class on their findings. English Text 3 reproduces some of the class notes students used to analyse the elements of the film:

English Text 3: Elements of kid pix

1 Social/economic reality

Quite simply some kids are shown as rich and some as poor. How is this shown? Which characters are the ones working, that is, serving the others? Do some characters expect to get their own way all the time? How does their social status make their life easier or more difficult? The film also presents that love can conquer any differences. Do you think this is realistic?

2 Disrespect for authority

Authority in most films is generally represented by people who are easy to identify. In spy films it could be represented by the President, or Prime Minister of the country, or even the Police Commissioner. In adventure films authority is represented by the police or by a special agent (e.g. Indiana Jones or Luke Skywalker). In horror films authority is at times represented by science or the church. In kid pix authority is represented by parents and teachers. What is the kids' reaction towards their parents and teachers? Is their disrespect justified? How different is their reality from yours?

3 Conformity

Teenagers always want to feel that they belong to a group or to society in general. This might explain why fashion and music are so important to teenagers. Which characters want to fit in but cannot in *Pretty in Pink*. What do you think is the problem that prevents them from doing so?

4 Rites of passage

The term 'rites of passage' refers to rituals that kids go through to show the rest of the world or themselves that they are grown up. Rites of passage occur in all societies. In Christian society baptism signifies a child's acceptance into the faith. In Aboriginal society there are specific ceremonies that children go through before they are considered adults. For example, boys are circumcised. Muslims must undertake a journey to Mecca at least once in their lifetime and following this they are called Hajis. In our society at large, 21st birthday parties signify that the birthday boy/girl is now an adult. Try to identify some of the rites of passage as portrayed in the film.

(Bill's class notes)

Texts such as these were important to the developing intertextuality of the students. Through such exercises they were learning to recognise not only the generic constructedness of the film but to describe the different stratagems by which it works on screen audiences. Work on romantic kid pix now involved more than an identification of sequences of stages. It involved consideration of abstract features of their representation (e.g. that young people are typically represented as 'conformist', as showing disrespect for authority and so on). Students were thus expanding their repertoire of ways of reflecting on/contextualising texts in this genre.

Of course, many of the students in this class needed assistance before they could apply these abstract categories. Bill amplified the meaning of unfamiliar terms such as 'conformism' and 'rites of passage' through examples from everyday life. The following exchange in English Text 4 represents a typical way of handling student difficulties with terminology:

English Text 4

Bill: Why do you wear the veil? [no response]. Mary's married. She's no longer single . . . she's been through the rite of passage of marriage. What big event does Andie face in the film?

Ranya: The Prom.

Bill: Yes, and what does that mean?

Ranya: Going out into the world . . .

Bill mediated the meaning-making practices of the culture (whether filmic, fictional or ceremonial) through making connections with what he knew would be familiar to students. Much of classroom interaction that I observed involved a shunting between familiar everyday experiences and semiotic abstractions – what in systemic functional linguistics would be called respectively 'token' and 'value'. This enabled students to oscillate between one level of abstraction (e.g. lived experience as 'token') and another (e.g. higher-order cultural meanings as 'value'). Work on modes of representation in *Pretty in Pink* made the class increasingly aware of film artifice – the fact that films create stereotypical versions of young people, of authority figures and of their relations. This awareness was manifested on a number of occasions of classroom talk.

While girls in this classroom came from a variety of linguistic, ethnic and religious backgrounds, almost half were from Arabic backgrounds, and were more attuned to the idea of the arranged marriage than to Hollywood notions of romantic love. This positioned them as resistant (or, at least, contradictory) subjects of films like *Pretty in Pink* and *Pretty Woman*. Following their viewing of the film *Pretty Woman* they talked about their reactions. An excerpt of this class discussion is reproduced in English Text 5:

English Text 5

Bill: The film is lovely, don't you think? [indistinguishable sounds of overall agreement about the film being great etc.]

Student 1: No, it isn't. It's not real. It . . .

Student 2: It makes you feel good sure. But it's a bit of a problem to show women like that – as weak and needing to be rescued.

Bill: Yes, Vivien was shown as submissive and vulnerable really.

            What do you others think?

Student 3:   She wasn't completely submissive. At the end she
decided to start a new life and . . .

Bill directed discussion of the representation of women in the film towards
students' work on the romance genre and how it can naturalise dubious
messages for today's women. Although he was focussing on textual practices
rather than on students' subjectivities, their contradictory experiences of
how life partnerships are formed provided them with a vantage point from
which to problematise *Pretty Woman*. Students discussed freely the issue
of romance versus arranged marriages and whether love really does
'conquer all differences'. And this informed their final deconstructive essay
on the role of romantic films in the continual oppression of women.

But before they could be expected to deal with a deconstructive essay
like this independently, they needed access to a prototype from which to
draw. English Text 6 is Bill's model essay which builds 'outwards' from
knowledge of the romance formula to discussion of its social implications
for today's woman. It is reproduced in full in order to demonstrate how he
uses knowledge about the genre as a launching pad for more deconstructive work. It serves as an exemplar of the trajectory from a specialised (and
perhaps reproductive) intertextuality to the more critical (and resistant)
intertextuality which had developed by the end of the unit.

English Text 6

'Despite its close adherence to the typical romantic formula, the film
Pretty Woman is a dangerous lesson for today's woman.' Discuss this
statement.

Pretty Woman does indeed adhere to all the rules of the romance
genre. This element of the film is crucial for both its plot development and for the audience's enjoyment of the film. In spite of this,
major concern has been expressed regarding the feeling of contentment generated by the film. It could be claimed that the film's
romantic ending where the modern princess is finally rescued by her
valiant prince is unrealistic in today's society and furthermore will
culminate in the perception that women are still passive, submissive
and expecting to be rescued by men.

The blockbuster film *Pretty Woman* certainly adheres to all the
rules of the romance genre. The two protagonists are strangers in the
beginning of the film and it is only when the debonair Edward (played
by Richard Gere) stops to ask directions from Vivien, the stunning
hooker with a heart of gold played by Julia Roberts, that they meet,

thus fulfilling the first identifiable stage of the romantic formula. This meeting results in the characters falling in love despite their opposing socio-economic backgrounds and diverse personalities. True to this very formula Vivien and Edward are in danger of losing their newly discovered love when he concludes his business dealings in Los Angeles. This 'losing' stage soon gives rise to the final ending, when Edward, the modern knight in shining armour, realises he cannot face his wealthy future without Vivien and comes to her rescue.

On the surface it might appear that this close adherence to the romance genre is only peripheral but in essence this characteristic of the film is crucial for the audience's enjoyment. Each event in the film is anticipated by the audience and in effect is very predictable. The famous shopping incident best exemplifies this. Vivien's ill treatment at the hands of the pretentious boutique owner is well contrasted with the treatment she receives the next day following Edward's intervention and is certainly anticipated by the audience.

Moreover the film has been so successful at the box-office because it consciously doesn't challenge the audience's understanding of romance. As a result, Edward's business partner serves as the customary 'baddie' and her friend provides the necessary contrast to convince all that Vivien is the most exemplary character just like the evil sisters in the universally loved 'Cinderella' make the latter appear superior, kind-hearted and virtuous.

Although the success of this escapist film might be considered plausible considering the world's economy is in recession, many critics have rejected the film as 'sentimental fluff'. Moreover they bitterly complain that its portrayal of the rich, handsome and wealthy male who comes to the rescue of the attractive, size 8 damsel, is anachronistic and unrealistic. This is indeed reinforced by the fact that Vivien's education and rescue from her street culture is not only undertaken by Edward but by another male, the hotel's maitre d'.

Notwithstanding the film's many fine qualities, including its diligent observation of the rules of the romance genre, it discloses ideas that are very traditional. These ideas mirror contemporary society's continual representation of women as passive, submissive and help-less – a most dangerous lesson indeed.

Bill Simon

Like Bill in his essay, these Year 9 students were increasingly shunting between one construal of the romance genre and another: specialised knowledge of its typical features and staging structure and more reflexive awareness of its role in naturalising 'dubious messages'. The students' final piece of writing demonstrates their increasingly fine-tuned awareness of romance semiosis, or romance meaning making. I did not manage to obtain a final copy of the essay so include only those portions of it that were jointly constructed in class at the end of the period during which I was present.

English Text 7: Final essay topic

'Some people maintain that romantic films are a testimony to the enduring power of love that can overcome all odds. Some others are adamant that the representation of both love and women in these films is unrealistic and furthermore that it will lead to the continual oppression of women.' What do you think?

Paragraph 1: The films *Pretty in Pink* and *Pretty Woman* are considered to be romantic because of their subject matter and their faithful following of the romantic formula. However, the manner in which women are portrayed in these films is quite problematic. Both Vivien in *Pretty Woman* and Andie in *Pretty in Pink* are presented as vulnerable, needy and dependent on men. The romance genre, as it is exploited in these two films, creates an unrealistic picture of today's women.

In this final work, students demonstrate an ability to turn the genre on its head, as it were, interpreting its 'social function' in new ways. The predictability of the very formula that students have learned to exploit in their own writing can now be seen to create and sustain 'an unrealistic picture of today's woman'. Students are now at a point where they can problematise the artifice of the romance narrative and challenge the interests and agendas of romance writers. To do this they draw on alternative discourses – some avowedly feminist and others made available from within their own lived experience of male–female relations. However, the critical intertextuality revealed in this last text fragment is (at least partly) an artefact of the specialised intertextuality through which they learned to analyse the romance genre in the first place.

Conclusion

The two case study classrooms demonstrate in different ways the principles outlined earlier and are foundational for development of a critical literacy.

First, both teachers offer their students alternating contextual frames by which to interpret what they learn. Their students have access to at least three construals of this: the applied (e.g. the cost of IVF; the meaning of terms such as 'rites of passage'), the theoretical (how the romance genre works; how inheritance affects an individual's characteristics) and the reflexive (the ethics of freezing embryos; the contribution of the romance genre to the oppression of women). Furthermore, there appears to be a hierarchy at work in students' control of these frames and associated inter-textualities: management of a critical frame is dependent on adequate induction into specialised frames. In other words, an effective critical inter-textuality is dependent on adequate development of a specialised intertextuality.

Second, their students are explicitly initiated into a metalanguage for reflecting on the texts they read and wrote – a metalanguage in which the category of genre plays a vital (albeit partial) role. In both the science and the English classrooms, students learn that genres package experience in identifiable and culturally normed ways, that they establish and presume a particular kind of relationship with their intended reader(s) and that they have a predictable global structure related to their social function(s). This meta-level awareness provides one pathway into the specialised intertextu-alities privileged in schooling. But it is also related quite explicitly to more critical forms of intertextuality.

In Margaret's class, students were increasingly able to draw on their knowledge of the field of human reproduction and its associated technolo-gies to reflect on issues facing consumers and to critique media representations of advances in these technologies (construed as 'cures'). They were able to manage this through writing a series of increasingly complex explanations. In Bill's class, students drew primarily on their knowledge of genre to critique the representation of women in filmic and fictional texts. The complexity his students faced was primarily semiotic and hence to do with controlling genre and related features, rather than ideational as with Margaret's students, where the challenge lay in control-ling the field of knowledge. But, in both classrooms, genre was a key to writing both specialised and critical texts.

Finally, both teachers recognise and assume responsibility for inducting students into the intertextualities privileged in their respective disciplines. The diverse starting points which many students have *vis à vis* educational learning means that at least some members of both classrooms do *not* share their teacher's assumptions about the goals, strategies and conse-quences of classroom work. Bill and Margaret play a crucial mediating role for such learners. For them, strategies like modelling, deconstruction and joint construction of text are essential if students are to construct an adequate picture of the demands of the secondary school learning context and to participate in the intertextualities it values. They are even more important in gaining control of critical intertextualities.

In sum, students who are dependent on their schooling to open up pathways into the territory of critical literacy profit well from pedagogies which make such pathways visible. It is important that those who already inhabit such territory do not hide from view the intensely demanding work many learners need to do as they develop the linguistic and other proficiencies on which a critical literacy depends.

Notes

1   The only examination which all New South Wales students face in the junior secondary years is the Year 10 Reference Test in English, Maths and Science. The English Test examines comprehension, interpretive and 'creative writing' skills. Examinees are always asked to interpret *and* produce literary or media texts (stories, poems, drama scripts and advertisements amongst other text types).
2   I am very grateful to both Margaret Watts and Bill Simon for the opportunity to visit their classrooms, to collect students' writing and to talk with them about the usefulness of the notions explored here.

References

Baker, C. and A. Luke (eds), 1991 *Towards a Critical Sociology of Reading Pedagogy: Papers of the XII World Congress on Reading.* Amsterdam: John Benjamins Publishing Company.

Ball, S., A. Kenny, and D. Gardiner, 1990 'Literacy, politics and the teaching of English', in I. Goodson and P. Medway (eds) *Bringing English to Order: The History and Politics of a School Subject* (Studies in Curriculum History Series; edited by I. Goodson). London: Falmer Press.

Callaghan, M. and J. Rothery, 1988 *Teaching Factual Writing: A Genre-Based Approach.* Sydney: Metropolitan East Disadvantaged Schools Program.

Christie, F., B. Devlin, P. Freebody, A. Luke, J. R. Martin, T. Threadgold, and C. Walton, 1991 *Teaching English Literacy: A Project of National Significance on the Preservice Preparation of Teachers for Teaching English Literacy.* 3 Volumes. Canberra: Department of Employment, Education and Training and Darwin, Centre for Studies of Language in Education, Northern Territory University.

Cranny-Francis, A. and J. R. Martin, 1995 'Writings/Readings: how to know a genre' in *Interpretations: Journal of the English Teachers' Association of Western Australia.* 28.3. pp. 1–32.

Fairclough, N. (ed.), 1992 *Critical Language Awareness* (Real Language Series). London: Longman.

Gee, J. P., 1990 *Social Linguistics and Literacies: Ideology in Discourses.* UK and USA, Falmer Press (in 'Critical Perspectives on Literacy and Education' series, edited by A. Luke).

Gilbert, P. 1993 '(Sub)versions: using sexist language practices to explore critical literacy', in *Australian Journal of Language and Literacy.* Victoria: Australian Reading Association.

Halliday M. A. K. and R. Hasan, 1985 *Language, Context and Text.* Geelong, Victoria, Deakin University Press (republished by Oxford University Press in 1989).

Hasan, R., 1995 'Literacy, everyday talk and society' in R. Hasan and G. Williams (eds) *Literacy in Society*. London: Longman, pp. 377–424.

Kress, G., 1989 *Linguistic Processes in Sociocultural Practice*. Oxford: Oxford University Press.

—— 1996 'Genre theory' in G. Bull and M. Anstey (eds) *The Literacy Lexicon*. Sydney, Prentice Hall, pp. 61–67.

—— 1997 *Before Writing: Rethinking the Paths to Literacy*. London and New York, Routledge.

Lankshear, C., 1994 'Critical literacy', Occasional Paper no. 3, *Australian Curriculum Studies Association*.

Lemke, J. L., 1985 'Ideology, intertextuality and the notion of register', in J. D. Benson and W. S. Greaves (eds) *Systemic Perspectives on Discourse, vol 1: Selected Theoretical Papers from the 9th International Systemic Workshop*. Norwood N.J.: Ablex, pp. 275–294.

Luke, A., 1992 'The social construction of literacy in the primary school', in Unsworth, L. (ed) *Literacy, Learning and Teaching: Language as Social Practice in the Classroom*. Melbourne: Macmillan.

Luke, A. 1995 'Genres of power', in R. Hasan and G. Williams (eds) *Literacy in Society*. London: Longman, pp. 308–338.

Luke, A., B. Comber and J. O'Brien, 1996 'Critical literacies and cultural studies', in G. Bull and M. Anstey (eds) *The Literacy Lexicon*. Sydney: Prentice Hall, pp. 31–46.

Macken-Horarik, M., 1995 'Literacy and learning across the curriculum: towards a model of register for secondary teachers' in R. Hasan and G. Williams (eds) *Literacy in Society*. London: Longman, pp. 232–278.

—— 1996 'Construing the invisible: specialized literacy practices in junior secondary English'. Unpublished PhD thesis. University of Sydney.

McRobbie, D., 1990 *Head Over Heels: Creative Writing through Romantic Fiction*. Melbourne, Longman Cheshire.

Martin, J. R., 1993 'Genre and literacy: modelling context in educational linguistics', *Annual Review of Applied Linguistics* 13, pp. 141–172.

Wallace, C., 1992a *Reading* (Language Teaching edited by C. N. Candlin and H. G. Widdowson). Oxford: Oxford University Press.

—— 1992b 'Critical language awareness in the EFL classroom', in N. Fairclough (ed), 1992 *Critical Language Awareness* (Real Language Series). London: Longman, pp. 59–92.

5

Telling tales out of school

Ray Misson

Everyone seems to be agreed that narrative is not only important, but somehow fundamental, basic and central to human life. Fredric Jameson speaks of 'the all-informing process of narrative' as 'the central function or instance of the human mind' (1981: 13).

Much of our life is bound up with stories. There are the stories in the newspaper in the morning, the stories the breakfast announcers are telling to entertain us (supposedly) as we drive into work, the stories in the advertisements we hear and see, stories often in the songs we listen to, stories students tell us, if we're teachers, about why they haven't got their work ready to hand in, stories we watch on TV (both factual and fictional ones), even stories sometimes in the books we read. There's no end to the stories we encounter every day.

And we produce stories all the time: telling people what has happened to us, what we want to have happen to us, why we didn't have time to do the work to hand in, stories to entertain our friends at dinner parties, stories we've heard elsewhere that confirm or shake our view of what the world is. Most importantly, we produce stories to tell ourselves, the stories through which we attempt to make sense of our experience, that we tell to confirm to ourselves that we are the kind of person that we want to be, stories that, in fact, produce the self in the telling and so make us what we are.

Stories have a social function too: they project to us aspects of the society we live in, and we subscribe to the implied vision they give of 'our' world and to the beliefs that go along with it. We are thus given a sense of belonging since we get confirmation that we are seeing the world as other people do. We can project to people our commitments through stories: 'I'm reading Anita Brookner's latest at the moment, but (with disparaging sneer) he's reading Stephen King!' You know a lot about how people see themselves and how they see the world through whether their favourite TV programme is *Seinfeld*, *Melrose Place* or *The Bill*.

There is not space to talk about all these kinds of stories in this chapter, obviously, so what I want to do is look at the work that can be done on stories in schools to prepare students for dealing with the stories they come in contact with out of school. The focus will be exclusively on fictional narratives. We will not be looking at news stories or biographies or personal anecdotes, but we will limit our investigation to the stories that are imagined and textually produced for leisure purposes, whether by Anita Brookner or Stephen King, by Jane Austen or Quentin Tarantino.

The class novel, the short story, the Shakespeare play, etc., all still have a significant place in the English curriculum, and more recently they have been joined by non-print texts – the film, the TV programme. The range in one sense is excellent, but what is often most striking is the disparity between the kind of narrative that is usually looked at in English classes, and the kind of narrative that students generally choose for their own leisure consumption outside school. I have argued fairly extensively in the past for the use of popular texts in the classroom, and I certainly stand by all those arguments (e.g. Misson, 1993a, 1993b, 1994a, 1994b). However, here I want to take a different tack. I want to look at the kind of work that can be done on narrative in schools, whatever the choice of text, to develop an understanding of how narrative operates. Students then can, and hopefully will, apply that understanding to other narrative texts they come across, either in school or out of it.

Even that is too big an agenda for a single chapter (indeed, perhaps for a lifetime), so the focus will be even more limited: it will be on some of the strategies that texts use to position their readers, to draw their readers in and make the readers invest in the images of the world they are being offered. Of course this focus has not been chosen at random: that question about how it is involving the reader is the most important question to ask about any text. There are a number of reasons for this, some of which have already been suggested.

We have already considered the importance of narrative in developing a sense of the self, how we try to understand our experience through turning it into a story we tell ourselves, thus becoming, in a very real sense, who we are through these stories. Beyond that, the stories we tell ourselves are influenced by the stories we are told: we model our stories on the stories others tell us. As a consequence, those stories, for better or worse, come to constitute our being, give us our sense of the person we are, or at least the person we would like to be. (You can have a *Melrose Place* mind in a body from *The Bill*, which is rather unfortunate and can prove something of a problem.) Still, the point stands that the way narrative provides frameworks through which we process our experience, measuring it up against the model provided by the narrative, makes that whole question of how we become involved in stories crucial.

The second point is that stories transmit culture, and so transmit ideology. Whether the story is a Shakespeare play, an Aboriginal myth, or *Seinfeld*, what is happening is that it is working to provide for us a model of what the world is like, and to seduce us into seeing the world in that particular way. Again, this makes the process by which we are drawn into the text and invited to acquiesce in the vision of the world as shown particularly significant. Understanding that process is obviously important in giving us better control over the text. It's going to allow us to get involved with the text more fully if we want to, and it's going to help us resist the text's operations on us if that's what we want to do.

These points are drawing on poststructuralist understandings of the centrality of language and texts in human life. In this framework, it becomes crucial to understand the ways in which texts position readers because it is through such positioning that we are, to a very large extent, created as human beings and given a sense of self (see Belsey, 1980; Silverman, 1983; Weedon, 1987; Cohan and Shires, 1988; Gee, 1990; Gilbert and Taylor, 1991; Misson, 1994c).

It is one of the central tenets of much poststructuralist thought that the self is created through the texts we are exposed to. 'Text' is being defined very broadly here as anything that can be read or interpreted for meaning, and so includes such things as the verbal texts produced anytime anyone speaks, visual texts, artefacts such as clothing and furniture, etc. These texts are made out of discourses, using the term in a way that stems from the work of Michel Foucault and that has been taken up by many others subsequently (see, for example, Foucault 1972; Weedon 1987; Gee 1990; Fairclough 1992; Gee 1992; Davies 1993; Lemke 1995). A discourse is the socially sanctioned way of talking about or representing or (in some definitions) doing something, a way which inevitably imports with it certain valuations, certain ways of thinking, a certain ideology. To take simple examples, there is a discourse of law, a discourse of education, a discourse of Christianity. When we are operating in one of these areas, we use a particular kind of language that constructs the world in particular ways and values particular things as important. The discourse assumes that the writer/speaker and the reader/listener are particular kinds of people and share particular values. That is, the discourse puts us, or attempts to put us, into a particular subject position; it creates a particular kind of subjectivity in us; it tries to make us the ideal originator or recipient of what is said and implied in the discourse. It does this more or less by assuming we will agree with it, offering its ideological shape as natural and beyond question (although we can, of course, resist). A text 'interpellates' (calls, hails), to use Althusser's term (1984), the reader into the subject position.

We should, however, talk in the plural of subject positions. Some texts are built out of a single discourse, especially things like legal texts which attempt to couch themselves restrictively in one discourse for the sake of explicitness, but in most texts, and especially artistic, narrative texts, there is usually a mix of discourses, and if there are multiple discourses operating simultaneously in the text, there are multiple subject positions that the reader is being called into. Some of them we accept, some of them we reject, because of our positioning in other discourses, since we always have available other discourses from the standpoint of which we might judge, if we wish, the discourses of the particular text we are reading. This makes reading, both reading the word and reading the world (to use Freire's famous phrase) a very complex matter (Freire, 1972; Freire and Macedo, 1987). Some would argue that our identity is constituted by the discourses we can partake in, and so by the set of subject positions that we can take up. Our complex identity is a matter of the complex configuration within us of multiple subjectivities.

Given this background, it is obviously important to understand the processes by which texts work to draw us into particular subject positions and become immersed in the world they are showing.

Tales told in school

Apart from its importance in helping us understand the way texts work on us, on a more mundane, practical level, to consider the mechanisms of textual positioning provides a strong framework for a lot of the work done on narrative in schools. It is worth considering for a moment the objectives of school work on fictional texts. Indeed, it is an interesting question why work on imaginative fiction is seen as so important in language and literacy learning. In curriculum documents, there are many purposes given, but they tend to come down to three, and historically, from the Greeks on, they are the three purposes that have always been given:

Working on texts can give us:

1 richer understanding of the world, i.e. it has a purpose of moral and emotional instruction;
2 a better understanding of texts in general to improve reading and writing practices, i.e. the purpose of the work is rhetorical;
3 greater pleasure in reading/viewing, i.e. the purpose is to enhance the entertainment given by the text.

Taking these one at a time:

A richer understanding of the world: moral and emotional instruction

Much of the work in English classes is geared around why the characters do what they do, and whether or not they are right to be doing it, or it is centred on the kind of thing the text is saying, the kind of human experience it is opening up to us, and the way that experience ought to be judged. To put it in the terminology I prefer, the purpose is ideological.

This is not something that English teachers ought to feel uncomfortable about. It is inevitable that once you start talking about narratives, you will start making value judgments about what the narrative is showing you, and if narratives have the kind of shaping significance in human life that everyone seems to agree they have, then you will also, if you are a teacher leading a discussion in a classroom, be working to fold into the subjectivity of your students a particular ideology. That seems obvious and inevitable: it is the game being played.

However, it does impose a great responsibility. Teachers need to be aware that this kind of ideological work is what they are doing, and not delude themselves that their work is value-neutral, that they are either 'just letting the text speak for itself' or 'just letting the students develop their own responses' (depending on the tradition they are working in). They need to be constantly bringing the values of the text explicitly up against their own values and their students' values, and they need to be constantly testing their own values against those that are coming up in the classroom either from the text or from their students.

One of the positive features of the emphasis on moral and emotional instruction in English teaching is how much excellent work has been done in English classes to promote attitudes that work against discrimination, whether on grounds of ethnicity or gender or, in more recent times, on grounds of sexuality. Their achievement in promoting feminist understanding in particular is something of which I think English teachers should be rather proud.

An understanding of how texts position us is central to this kind of work that is concerned with ethical and emotional understanding. One of the things we will want students to be able to do is to analyse what a text wants its reader to believe. Texts do a lot of their ideological work by positioning us, and putting us through particular emotional and intellectual processes.

A better understanding of texts to improve reading and writing practices: rhetorical purpose

Much of the work on narrative in English classrooms, as various studies have shown, is very much locked into that first purpose of explicating the moral and emotional meaning of the work. It is sometimes felt that analysis of technique is inherently boring, although, curiously, the one area where teachers do seem to be doing such work is with film. Teachers who would hesitate to talk about the way a sentence is constructed or the way the narrative point of view shifts will happily start talking about long shots or the difference between high and low camera angles when they start analysing films.

Even so, there is an implicit belief that in the work on a text ways of reading are being modelled and therefore taught, although it seems to be generally believed that there is no need to be explicit about this: it will just be communicated through the modelling. Similarly, the texts read are often used as a starting point for students' own 'creative' writing, although, again, there is rarely much technical analysis of the model text undertaken as a foundation on which the students might build. Of course, I would argue that, for purposes of developing both reading and writing skills, there is a need to work at an explicit theoretical level to promote a surer understanding of the nature of textuality. Theoretical analysis provides understanding that is generalisable to other texts, thus helping students get better control of them. It teaches them the questions to ask of the texts they read, and it helps develop their understanding and control of writing strategies when they are producing texts of their own.

The work I am doing in this chapter is largely within the area covered by this second purpose, and I hope my practice here will demonstrate the usefulness and the pleasures of working in this way.

Greater pleasure in reading/viewing: purpose of entertainment

This is a big issue. I think it needs to be said that the kind of pleasure one takes in reading a text at home for leisure purposes is quite different from the pleasures possible in working on the text in school. The particular kind of immediate involvement of private reading or viewing cannot be recreated in the classroom, and it is ridiculous to believe that work on the text there can be based in any sustained way on that sort of immediate private pleasure. This is the fundamental problem underlying a lot of the overly subjective, impressionistic work ostensibly stemming from the reader-response movement that can be seen in many classrooms: such work is not acknowledging the very different mode of reading that occurs as soon as you bring a text into the classroom. Enjoyable work on texts in classrooms comes from reflection and analysis, from seeing more in the text, things not noticed on first reading, seeing different possibilities that the sharing of different readings in the class builds up. It comes from the interest in seeing how the text is working. People, curiously to me, seem to think that analysis lessens the enjoyment, but if we like something, we inevitably want to know more about it. If one thinks of most students (most people) who have a favourite singer, actor or film director. They will read all they can of background material. They will read quite technical analyses of their work in magazines and feel that they are getting closer to the texts and what it is they love about them. There is no reason why it should be different with the texts in school.

In particular, it is important that students should analyse the ways in which the text is producing pleasure, because giving pleasure is a fundamental way a text has of positioning the reader. But also, analysing the sources of pleasure in the text is a way of keeping in mind that the text does have entertainment value, something that, unfortunately, is often lost in class work.

The work on texts in the classroom aims at bringing into greater awareness the texts' strategies in any or all of these three areas. Here I am clearly working with a model of teaching about narrative texts that is aiming at explicitness, and moving away from loose notions of personal response that still, surprisingly given the critiques mounted, underpin a great deal of the work on texts in schools. This notion of 'response' is so problematic that it is worth digressing for a moment to consider it.

Digression on response

'Response' is a word to be distrusted, because it has become an empty sign for 'doing the right thing in text-based English classes'. Whatever any teacher wants to do, however they want to teach, they simply have to say that they are basing it on the students' response to the text and their practice seems to be automatically validated. Readings coming from almost any critical school of thought can be given the imprimatur of being based on 'response' (see Tompkins, 1980; Corcoran and Evans, 1987; Freund, 1987; Beach, 1993). Although the contention rarely surfaces, the word is a site in which deep conflicts about the nature of text study in the classroom can be and are played out.

Some of the axes on which there are differences are

immediate v. considered
emotional v. logical
inchoate v. expressed
private v. public
intuitive/natural v. ideological/ethical

There is also a three-way division, or hierarchy, with expository work flanked on either side by different kinds of evaluation:

reactive-evaluative v. expository v. critical-evaluative

In a great deal of talk about response, the first term in the pairs and in the triad is the one that is valued in the curriculum rhetoric, the other ones those that are valued (and rightly so) when response enters the practical world of assessment. There is a myth of the initial response being transcendentally pure and personal, a direct unmediated communion with the text, the glory of which can only be dimmed by subsequent intellectualisation about it. We tend to distrust the final written response, unless it can give us the inevitably false impression that we are getting the pure unmediated 'personal voice' coming through. (I remember vividly in an examination moderating session once arguing with a person who seemed to take gram-matical correctness as a sign of glibness, and grammatical awkwardness as a sign that the student was 'honestly struggling with the text'.)

Many writers have provided a strong critique of the limitations of what is generally acceptable and accepted in text classrooms, and of the incontro-vertible fact that 'personal voice' is a textual construct that has little to do with providing access to the soul of the writer (see, e.g. Gilbert 1989). It is worth stressing, moreover, that much of the valued work on texts (work valued by students as well as by teachers) is not a product of the untram-melled free reaction model. The most exciting work in text classrooms comes in discussion when students and teachers work together and discover things about the text that the students, and probably the teacher, did not perceive on their first reading. An anecdotal example that comes readily to mind concerns one of the favourite texts for study in the final year of secondary English in Victoria, David Malouf's novel, *Fly Away Peter*. A number of teachers have commented on their experience that their students read the book and did not like it, but then became really excited about it when they started working on it in class and began to see the thematic and symbolic patterns grow. By the end the students were saying that it was one of their favourite books. Their initial reaction had been totally overturned, and yet some of them will not have sat down and read the book right through again. This suggests that in the text response classroom, the initial reading may provide basic material to be worked on in terms of starting to become familiar with the narrative and getting initial reactions to characters and to the book as a whole, but this basic material is usually less important in itself than the work that is subsequently done on it as it is reshaped and added to in further thinking about and rereading of sections of the text. There is a belief with some teachers and a lot of students that subsequent work is a move away from the ideal purity of the immediate response in the initial reading experience. However, I would argue that with most complex texts (and we value complexity) the response that comes after we have thought through and mentally knocked the material into shape is the one that usually matters. It is surely true that reading a book, even for pleasure rather than teaching purposes, is not finished when one reads the last word, but there is a mental reconsideration and restructuring of the textual mate-rial that goes on as we replay certain interesting parts over in our minds, and as we mull over what it was all about and what we thought of it and why it had the effect it did. We can (and often do) even come to the conclu-sion that it was a better book or a worse book than we took it for when actually reading it. Teachers undoubtedly hope that the work on texts in class gives students strategies and capabilities so that they can develop more sophisticated complex responses in their initial reading. Nevertheless, it is necessary to get away from privileging the seeming purity of the undiscussed response so often. It does less than justice to the work teachers and students do in class in developing strong and diverse understandings of the texts they read.

The conflicting messages being given to students is the major concern if we maintain a rhetoric of open response. It is constantly implied that the basis of the text work is the student's 'honest' response, what they 'really feel' about the text, whereas often what is in fact meant and communicated in practice is that text work is based on a particular kind of response to a particular kind of text. Not any response and not any text will do. It is because of this that explicitness in analysis is important, both to ensure that students understand the game that is being played, but also to give them better understanding of what 'response' actually might consist of when dealing with a text. The energising impulse behind much work on text is indeed the affective involvement generated, and this should be nurtured, developed and renewed, but in itself it is neither above questioning nor usually sufficient to sustain the extended work on a text in the classroom of any of the three kinds outlined above.

Strategies for positioning readers

To return to our specific concern with narrative texts and how they position readers, I would argue that, in the end, the only reason for involving ourselves with texts for leisure purposes is the pleasure that we get out of them. Pleasure is, of course, a massively difficult concept to theorise, linked as it often is to the equally problematical concept of desire. There are all kinds of pleasures, from the obvious simple ones of feeling good through being made to laugh, to pleasures due to having our conception of the world stretched and changed and so feeling that we have somehow extended ourselves, to the darker pleasures of having had the opportunity to rehearse negative or transgressive emotions vicariously through our reading. Our desires are multifarious, and the pleasures that come from fulfilling them through reading or viewing texts will inevitably be every bit as varied.

Even more varied and multifarious is the self, as we have seen. If we are made up of many selves – multiple subjectivities – then the texts we read can draw on this whole repertoire of selves to find an answering response. Different parts of our being – different selves – are being called on when we are reading a novel by George Eliot than when we are reading one by Toni Morrison. The two texts are working with a different range of desires, giving different pleasures, and, of course, in doing so, modifying that collection of selves – the multiple subjectivities – that we think of as our self.

I would argue that there are basically two ranges of desire that texts call on: the desire for intense experience and the desire for confirmation. The first is unsettling, the second is settling, and, of course, all texts that we consider successful work with both desires. We would not be interested in a text that did not give us an emotional or intellectual experience at least more intense than sitting around in our room doing nothing, and we would reject a text that did not strike any chords that it was showing the world as we see it, or, in a few life-changing cases, as the text itself has made us revise our vision of it.

The classic structure of narrative ensures that both desires are satisfied. If we take that structure in its simplest form as 'orientation – complication – resolution', then a traditional narrative moves us from stasis, through a dynamic section where the stasis is disrupted, back to a (modified) stasis. Thus the classic text begins with confirmation, takes us through a disruption that gives us an intense experience, and then brings us back to a revised confirmation. In many of the texts that we value most, that process will have been revelatory, the revision in our way of thinking that is confirmed at the end will have been significant for us. But we ought not to despise those texts in which an expected story is played out, and we are simply confirmed in the same set of values at the end. They can give pleasure too.

Texts work with these desires in different ways. Playing on the desire for confirmation, they can

1 assume a common framework of knowledge, priorities and beliefs; or
2 unsettle our certainties and then reaffirm them, perhaps in a revised form (we have just been discussing this, so we won't return to it explicitly later).

Playing on the desire for intense experience they can at the level of the story:

3 put us in particular relationship with the various characters;
4 make us want certain things to happen because they promise an intense experience;
   or, working at what we might call the aesthetic level, they can
5 provide us with an experience of meaningful ordering.

(Note that I don't say that the experience is necessarily emotional, because I think it can often be intellectually oriented, and note that I've avoided the word 'vicarious' because I would not want for a moment to suggest that there is anything sneaky or sordid or second best about this.)

In terms of positioning us, the basic questions that one can ask corresponding to each of these two major areas in which we become involved in texts are:

1 What is the text assuming that we know and/or value (since this is a necessary condition for the text's providing confirmation); and
2 What kind of experience is the text offering us, and what is its purpose in putting us through that experience?

Of course, in a classroom one would not ask those questions bluntly in those terms, but they are the crucial questions one often finds oneself asking in modified form, in terms appropriate to particular texts.

Confirmation: common framework of knowledge, priorities and beliefs

To consider the question, 'What is the text assuming that we know and/or value?', as an example take the opening words of a story:

It was one of those days when . . .

which is a very powerful opening gesture. It is so powerful because it is assuming common knowledge and common experience between the narrator and the reader. It is saying, 'You and me, we know about those kinds of days. . . . ' It is inviting the reader to contribute to the text, to work her/his own experience into it, and so make some kind of investment in it. It might continue:

It was one of those days when thunder lurks around, and you know it's going to break the clouds wide open by the time nightfall comes.

or

It was one of those days when the hedgerows suffused the countryside with a particular sweetness, as Emily Manion arrived in Bentmore to take up her job at the local hospital.

or

It was one of those days when you knew from the moment you got up that the shit was sure as hell going to hit the fan.

In these cases, it is evident how the assumption of common knowledge locates the reader in a particular kind of perception, a way of seeing the world. This is done, of course, not just or even particularly by drawing on our worldly experience, but by creating and utilising generic expectations. We are in each case as readers clearly lodged in a particular genre, and so we are contributing our generic understanding to the construction of the piece. We can already be pretty sure of the kind of world that is going to be developed in this story, and the kind of values that are going to be significant. The first one is in a suspense/horror genre: we are the kind of people who expect the natural world to be sympathetic to the movements within the lives of people or of the supernatural. The second one is a Mills and Boon romance; we are open to the loveliness of the English country-side and relate it to the innocence of Nurse Emily Manion, who is undoubtedly about to meet a tall dark and arrogant chief surgeon. The third one is a crime/detective story, where things go wrong and a high value is placed on instinct and resourcefulness to cope with it.

It is often said that popular texts are easy to read because they do every-thing for the reader. This is true in one way, but not true in another. The texts are often not very detailed, indeed rather sketchy. What is happening is that they are working within clear generic frameworks, and so we as readers can supply very easily the things that are necessary to fill out the world of the text. This is one of the reasons why they can be so absorbing: they don't make us work very hard because the things they are asking from us are easy to supply from our generic understanding, but we are actually ourselves contributing an immense amount to the text, and to that degree investing in it. The comparative emptiness of the text is an invitation to fill it with our own culturally generated understanding and certainly our fantasies, and if we answer the invitation to give those things, then we are hooked.

More complex texts make us work harder and involve us in more interesting ways, although not necessarily more powerfully. Take what is probably the most famous opening sentence in English literature:

> It is a truth universally acknowledged, that a single man in possession of a good fortune, must be in want of a wife.
>
> (Austen, 1972 (1813): 51)

This is particularly cunning because it seems to be explicitly stating the framework of assumptions, the common experience between narrator and reader, but, of course, it is more deeply involving because we see that the statement is ironic. 'Other people act as if it is a truth universally acknowledged, but you, dear reader, and I know better and understand the kind of ludicrous and reprehensible behaviour such people indulge in. We can stand back and laugh at the foolishness of these people,' one of whom we immediately see, Mrs Bennet. We are thus again drawn into a particular complicity of viewpoint, of understanding, with the narrator, all the more strongly because the irony implies a kind of superiority in our perception and so in our values.

Take another famous opening (at least in the Australian context), that of Henry Lawson's short story 'The Drover's Wife':

> The two-roomed house is built of round timber, slabs, and stringy bark, and floored with split slabs. A big bark kitchen standing at one end is larger than the house itself, verandah included.
>
> Bush all round – bush with no horizon, for the country is flat. No ranges in the distance. The bush consists of stunted, rotten native apple trees. No undergrowth. Nothing to relieve the eye save the darker green of a few sheoaks which are sighing above the narrow almost waterless creek. Nineteen miles to the nearest sign of civilisation – a shanty on the main road.
>
> The drover, an ex-squatter, is away with sheep. His wife and children are left here alone.
>
> (1986 (1892): 19)

It is worth noting the amount of cultural knowledge encoded in this passage

– knowledge about living conditions in late-nineteenth-century Australia, knowledge about the bush – so that we can immediately place the kind of poverty and hardship these people are living under. But it is also important to note the way in which the reader is being positioned. The description is, of course, written in a fairly notational style, not unlike the description of a setting for a play. The most obvious stylistic feature is the present tense, which is maintained right through the story. It is often said (by students anyway) that this makes the story more immediate, and perhaps it does in a way, but its major effect is to keep our view objective, and so, in fact, to distance us. We are very conscious of standing with the narrator observing, if already feeling the weight of destitution. We will return to 'The Drover's Wife' later, and look at the use made of this narrative stance at the climax of the story.

The attraction of the kind of involvement based on common under-standing, as I have said, is that of confirmation. We all of us have a broad repertoire of attitudes, of possible selves, and when we are brought into texts in this way, we have the pleasure of finding that the text is confirming that this is a reasonable and acceptable, indeed natural and desirable way of seeing the world. Even more than seeing things as we do, texts often see them with greater clarity than we can command since they don't have all the messy complexity of human beings who have to get up in the morning and meet the diffuse demands of everyday life. They can give us a focussed, clear view that we may find true and/or attractive because all the mess has been stripped away. This is certainly true of popular genres. The attraction is the fantasy of a comparatively simple world where the ideals that are buried for us under the weight of mundanity are able to be lived by. There are, of course, plenty of cases where we resist the text's invitation to involve ourselves. We don't fall for the text's strategy: we aren't led to take on the assumptions because they don't conform to one of our possible selves, or at least not one we find it desirable to develop. In these circumstances, Jane Austen seems impossibly quaint, Lawson seems clichéd and sentimental. There is nothing reprehen-sible about this, of course. It means that we don't become subject to that particular view of the world, which might be a good thing. But then, on the other hand, it might mean that we miss a great deal of pleasure and an extension of our possible perception.

Let us now turn to look at the way texts involve us by playing on that second desire: the desire for intense experience.

Intense experience: relationship with characters

Certainly one of the ways in which this is worked with, is by making us relate in particular ways to various characters, although the processes through which this happens are much more complex than a lot of the easy talk about identification suggests (see Davis, 1987: 125–136). Our involve-ment with characters is a complex mixture of observation, identification and attraction.

We are of course positioned differently in relation to different characters and so the dynamic of how we interact with them varies. One of the simplest variables is the matter of how much we have access to their thoughts. In *Pride and Prejudice*, for example, we have almost total access to Elizabeth's thoughts, but virtually no direct access to Jane's. If Jane Austen wants us to know what is going on for Jane, she either has Elizabeth speculate on it, or has a conversation between the two in which Jane can tell us herself. This inevitably suggests to us that Elizabeth is a far more interesting person than Jane, and that it may be all very wonderful to be quiet, demure and self-effacing, but it's better to have the spirit and intelligence of Elizabeth. (You get a richer, sexier husband in the end, anyway, which just goes to confirm it.)

It depends too on how much we see things through the eyes of a partic-ular character. We have a great deal of access to the Drover's Wife's thoughts, but we tend to be observing her, rather than seeing with her. Some of the strongest characters in literature indeed are developed quite externally – Catherine and Heathcliff in *Wuthering Heights*, for example. We see amazingly individual and strong personalities, performing them-selves in front of us, but they always retain a kind of mystery because we do not have direct access to what is going on in their minds. We only have the outward articulation and performance of it.

There is a superb moment in George Eliot's *Middlemarch* where she makes us aware of how naturalised the whole business of seeing the action focused through a particular character is. It's about a third of the way through the (very long) book:

> One morning, some weeks after her arrival at Lowick, Dorothea – but why always Dorothea? Was her point of view the only possible one with regard to this marriage? I protest against all our interest, all our effort at understanding being given to the young skins that look blooming in spite of trouble; for these too will get faded, and will know the older and more eating griefs which we are helping to neglect. In spite of the blinking eyes and white moles objectionable to Celia, and the want of muscular curve which was morally painful to Sir James, Mr Casaubon had an intense consciousness within him, and was spiritually a-hungered like the rest of us.
>
> (1965 (1871–2): 312)

She then goes on to develop her great analysis of what is going on for Casaubon, which doesn't make us particularly like him, but certainly makes us realise his complexity and the ways in which he is pitiable. Notice in the passage quoted George Eliot's way of assuming common experience with the reader, and so positioning us very powerfully within a particular framework of humanist values as people who acknowledge and understand the desire for spiritual, emotional fulfilment. And notice too how this passage places the subsequent development of Casaubon in a particular moral framework. We are to read it as confirming the centrality of a particular kind of intense consciousness which can be equated with spiritual hunger.

Non-print texts equally position us with particular characters. You might think, for example, of how in *Seinfeld* we are positioned differently in relation to Jerry than we are to the other characters. We tend to be led to see things with Jerry, whereas we observe the other characters going through their paces. That, for most people, makes the other characters more interesting than Jerry himself, because more outlandish (see Misson, 1995: 66–67 for fuller discussion).

As a more detailed example, take the opening sequence of Elia Kazan's film of John Steinbeck's *East of Eden* (1954). After the credit sequence and a scene-setting written description contrasting Salinas and Monterey, we see the figure of a middle-aged woman (Jo Van Fleet), tightly clad in black, walking along the street of seaside Monterey. She passes by a young man, sitting on the wooden sidewalk, who tensely under lowered eyebrows looks up at her, with the kind of pained vulnerable intensity only James Dean was capable of. She goes into the bank, where it is established that she is madam of one of the town's brothels and a scandalous figure to respectable ladies, although marked by a no-nonsense businesswoman toughness in her interactions with the bank. When she leaves, the young man follows her back to her house.

Clearly, when one sees it, everything is working to bring the audience into immediate sympathy with the James Dean character, Cal: the way that he is often seen in close-up, shot from a low angle to increase the power of his presence; the fact that it is his point of view that we seem to be seeing because the editing keeps on, in the usual way of cinematic grammar, cutting from him looking to what he is seeing; the way that the music creeps in to articulate his inner state whenever we see him whereas the music soundtrack tends to be silent when the woman is on the screen. All this means that there is no doubt as to who we are meant to sympathise with, and that we are meant to value passionate youthful intensity more than the tight repression of natural feeling that we sense in that black-clad figure.

We can use this scene as an example of the second way in which narrative texts work with our desire for intense experience.

Intense experience: making us want certain outcomes

Texts make us want certain things to happen because they promise an intense experience. There are a number of ways in which they do this. The first thing they do is establish narrative questions that we want the answers to, and this keeps us reading or viewing.

In *East of Eden*, for example, we are immediately set up to ask what is the relationship between the James Dean and Jo Van Fleet characters, and since there is all this emotion surging around in the Dean character, what will be the outcome of some climactic meeting between them. We probably hypothesise, since emotion between a young man and an older woman usually stems from a mother–son relationship, that she is his mother, and, of course, that raises all sorts of questions about how they got into their current situation. It is worth noting how much these questions establish for us what it is we are to look for and value. We are immediately located by them in a world in which personal relations, and probably family relations, are central, in a world where what matters is emotions, not, for example, the problems of prostitution in seaside towns, or a contrast between agricultural and fishing economies and ways of life. Prostitution and the contrast between Salinas and Monterey are both there to shape our response to the emotional story, and to help position us in certain attitudes about what are good emotions and what are bad, or more to the point, what are attractive intense emotions that we would like to have ourselves and that we can participate in through the text, and what are worthless ones we can despise.

When a narrative question is established, we expect an answer, and will be cheated if we don't get one, or if that expectation is not somehow dealt with and diverted. Similarly, if we see some sort of unresolved situation, we will want and expect resolution. Thus there is expectation of a showdown between James Dean and Jo Van Fleet. Texts will withhold the fulfilment of the expectation for a time, and so make our desire all the stronger. Of course, there are all sorts of stories, and the things that can call for resolution are of many different kinds, as can be the kind of resolution that they make us want. They may make us want to see people going through intricate emotional shifts, and see relationships either resolved or break down; they may make us want disasters to happen to people. We may dread them at one level perhaps, but want them at another, as in tragedies.

We can also be positioned to want certain developments in a text by the creation of a pattern that, once established, we will feel cheated if we don't see played out. The film, *Seven*, for example, creates a pattern that is incomplete until there has been a murder based on all seven of the deadly sins. The audience is positioned both to want the pattern to be completed, and for the main characters to succeed in stopping the pattern; indeed, we would feel cheated if all seven were not played out. But the interesting feature of the film is that the expectation that somehow the pattern will be turned back on the criminal and he will suffer from it is in fact part of the criminal's plan, and so the pattern one might have expected is played out, but with a different meaning and emotional charge. Of course, the other pattern of expectation built up through the unresolved issues in the relationship between the Brad Pitt character and his wife, indeed in the Brad Pitt character altogether, reach resolution here and make us ready to accept the inevitability of the ending we get.

The pattern that is created is often generic. When we heard about Nurse Emily Manion arriving in Bentmore, we knew immediately what to expect: a tall dark and arrogant surgeon who in the end will turn out not to be so arrogant. The fascinating thing is that as soon as on page 3, we read,

> 'What kind of fool left these bags in the corridor?'
> Emily turned in surprise and found herself facing a tall white-coated figure. A pair of intense blue eyes burned at her in anger.

the fascinating thing is that, if we're romance readers, we don't say 'Oh God, not again,' but rather 'Yes, here he is!' There is a great deal of pleasure in the predictable, and popular genres work on this. Not only popular genres of course. We have a similar reaction when Elizabeth Bennet meets Darcy, when Jane Eyre meets Rochester. Of course, whether it is Nurse Emily Manion or Elizabeth Bennet, there is an inherent ideological message about the desirability of marriage as an outcome, about the finest destiny a woman can have being the simultaneous taming of and submission to a dominant man, although I think it misleading simply to say that the two books are ideologically identical. The same message is couched in rather different terms, and so is modified in each case. The point is that the emotional engagement we have, that desire for this particular outcome, does lodge us in a particular ideology, and very powerfully so, since our emotions are invested in it.

In all of these cases, the crucial thing is that our questions are answered, our expectations fulfilled, our uncertainties resolved, although maybe not in the way we expect. We tend to value more highly texts which can surprise us by giving us the satisfaction of closure, but in a way that we didn't foresee.

Intense experience: meaningful ordering

There are, of course, texts that don't lead us through to that kind of resolution, but if we are to find them satisfying, we must think that they have fulfilled their purpose, perhaps a purpose of presenting a fragmented, uncertain world or consciousness. We want intensity of experience within a meaningful framework. By setting us up to want certain kinds of actions, by making us go through certain emotional processes, texts promise that intensity to us.

The emotional shape of the text, the sequence of feeling we go through can be different from the story, or rather, the story can be shaped and told to produce a particular emotional effect. 'The Drover's Wife' is a story in which what we might call the aesthetic shape is very powerfully deployed to position the reader. On a story level, the narrative is shaped around the killing of the snake that is sighted at the beginning of the story, and killed at the end. But, on what we might call the aesthetic level, what we have, told very objectively, is a sequence of incidents that build up a picture of the life of this woman. As we noted before, the story is largely in the present tense, which has an objectifying effect: we stand with the narrator observing this woman. Finally she kills the snake:

> She lifts the mangled reptile on the point of her stick, carries it to the fire, and throws it in; then piles on the wood and watches the snake burn. The boy and dog watch, too. She lays her hand on the dog's head, and all the fierce, angry light dies out of his yellow eyes. The younger children are quieted, and presently go to sleep. The dirty-legged boy stands for a moment in his shirt, watching the fire. Presently he looks up at her, sees the tears in her eyes, and, throwing his arms around her neck, exclaims:
> 'Mother, I won't never go drovin'; blast me if I do!'
> And she hugs him to her worn-out breast and kisses him; and they sit thus together while the sickly daylight breaks over the bush.
>
> (Lawson 1986 (1892): 26)

The ending is so moving because the reader has been positioned so thoroughly as an observer, and we don't expect our sympathy to gain articulation in the story. The boy's unexpected words catch up and articulate all the feeling that has been generated in the reader, and so provide an enormous emotional release. It is a superbly structured piece of writing.

Or think of Quentin Tarantino's *Pulp Fiction*. The complicated time sequence there clearly has a number of purposes, but one of its main ones is to maintain a comic ambience, which positions us in a particular way with regard to the often violent action. The film moves to a resolution with Vincent and Jules having successfully got through a difficult time, leaving the cafe to fairly jaunty music. It is an image of comic success. We know rationally that in fact Vincent is going to be killed before long because we've seen it happen, but our experience of watching the film is that Vincent goes through an awful lot of shit, including being killed, and comes out all right. Our sense of emotional structure will always dominate over our sense of the chronological sequence. Think of the different effect the film would have had if the events had been presented chronologically: it would have been a very much darker, as well as a very much more episodic and fragmented film. We would probably read it as a moral tale about how those who live by the gun, die by the gun.

Questioning Tarantino

Pulp Fiction is the kind of text that is extremely popular out of school, and so I want to finish by looking specifically at a section of it, examining how it is positioning its viewers, and trying out on it some of the questions and categories that have been set up in this chapter.

I have chosen *Pulp Fiction* because it seems to be a central text for the generation now in secondary schools, in spite of the fact that it is R-rated – age 18 and over (not that that means anything in these days of video). When the Australian national government-run rock radio station, Triple J, held a survey of the hundred best films of all time in 1996, *Pulp Fiction* came out on top, which perhaps shows that Triple J listeners see 'all time' as a rather limited period, but does also suggest that this is a significant text for a particular age group. In fact, I am sure when we look back it will be seen as a key text of the nineties. It, of course, cannot be worked on much in schools because it is R-rated, but for that very reason, I want to show the importance of developing in students the habit of asking questions about how the text is engaging us, and how it is positioning us, not particularly for purposes of resisting the text, but rather to get a clearer view of the pleasure and the way of seeing the world that it is offering.

I want to analyse what is probably the second most famous sequence in the film. I decided against looking at the most famous – the adrenalin shot to the heart – since it's harder to analyse for those who don't know the film because one needs to look at the build-up. Instead, I want to look at the sequence in which Vincent and Jules don't get shot, and someone else does. This is the beginning of the third of the three inner stories. We have already seen near the beginning, Jules and Vincent come to the apartment and terrorise and kill two of the three young men there, but we didn't know there was a fourth hiding in the bathroom. Now we see the climax of this interaction again, but initially from the point of view of the fourth man in the bathroom. After Jules has shot the second of the men, he is introducing Vincent to the third man, Marvin, cowering in a corner, who it seems is an acquaintance of his, when

The bathroom door bursts open and the Fourth Man charges out, silver Magnum raised, firing six booming shots from his hand cannon.

FOURTH MAN

Die . . . die . . . die . . . die! . . .

Dolly into Fourth Man. He screams until he's dry firing. Then, a look of confusion crosses his face.

TWO SHOT – JULES AND VINCENT

standing next to each other, unharmed. Amazing as it seems, none of the Fourth Man's shots appear to have hit anybody. Jules and Vincent exchange looks like, 'Are you hit?' They're as confused as the shooter. After looking at each other, they bring their looks up to the Fourth Man.

                              FOURTH MAN
I don't understand.

The Fourth Man is taken out of the scenario by the two men's bullets who, unlike his, hit their marks. He drops dead.

The two men lower their guns. Jules, obviously shaken, sits down in a chair. Vincent, after a moment of respect, shrugs it off. Then heads toward Marvin in the corner.

                              VINCENT
Why the fuck didn't you tell us about that guy in the bathroom? Slip your mind? Forgot he was in there with a goddam hand cannon?

                              JULES
                            (to himself)
We should be fuckin' dead right now.
                             (pause)
Did you see that gun he fired at us? It was bigger than him.

                              VINCENT
.357

                              JULES
We should be fuckin' dead!

                              VINCENT
Yeah, we were lucky.

Jules rises, moving toward Vincent.

                              JULES
That shit wasn't luck. That shit was somethin' else.

Vincent prepares to leave.
                              VINCENT
Yeah, maybe.

                              JULES
That was . . . divine intervention. You know what divine intervention is?

                              VINCENT
Yeah, I think so. That means God came down from heaven and stopped the bullets.

                              JULES
Yeah, man, that's what it means. That's exactly what it means! God

came down from heaven and stopped the bullets.

VINCENT

I think we should be going now.

JULES

Don't do that! Don't fuckin' do that! Don't blow this shit off! What just happened was a fuckin' miracle!

VINCENT

Chill the fuck out, Jules, this shit happens.

JULES

Wrong, wrong, this shit doesn't just happen.

VINCENT

Do you wanna continue this theological discussion in the car, or at the jailhouse with the cops?

JULES

We should be fuckin' dead now, my friend! We just witnessed a miracle, and I want you to fuckin' acknowledge it!

VINCENT

Okay man, it was a miracle, can we leave now?

(Tarantino, 1994: 137–139)

They do leave and they do continue their 'theological discussion' in the car. Jules is driving. Vincent is sitting in the front passenger seat, still holding his gun. Marvin is sitting in the back. Jules has undergone a religious conversion and is going to quit being a gunman. At a certain point in the argument with Jules,

Vincent turns to the back seat with the .45 casually in his grip.

VINCENT

Marvin, what do you make of all this?

MARVIN

I don't even have an opinion.

VINCENT

C'mon, Marvin. You gotta have an opinion. Do you think God came down from heaven and stopped the bullets?

Vincent's .45 goes BANG!

(Tarantino, 1994: 141)

We see the back window of the car suddenly spattered with blood and what one can only imagine is bits of Marvin's skull and brains.

The kind of positioning that's going on here is obviously very complex and subtle, not least because of the multiple ironies involved. People when they start talking about the values in a text, often go immediately to the action and the characters, and see them as a model that readers will emulate, but, of course, our positioning, as we've seen, is developed in much more complex and varied ways. In terms of the characters here, we are certainly positioned to relate to Jules and Vincent, since they are leading characters, and not expendable extras. Besides, their particular brand of cool – the nonchalant professionalism with which they go about their job as hitmen – is much more attractive than the sweaty nervousness of their victims. But there is more than that going on. Jules and Vincent are both, in their different ways, rather stupid. Professional thugs in most movies tend to be taciturn killing machines: Jules and Vincent talk a great deal, and often not particularly intelligently. John Travolta as Vincent is also obviously ageing and has rather let himself go, so the character may be attractive, and we feel kindly disposed towards him, but we do not particularly identify with him. It's not surprising to us that he lets his gun go off accidentally since there is a history of incompetence, although there is no denying the shock when it happens. There is, of course, an air of comic unreality about much of the sequence, a sense of it being a game, as we can see in such things as the way Jules and Vincent look at each other after they've been shot at, and then the unison, choreographed raising of the guns to shoot the fourth man. So, we are involved with the characters, but kept at an ironic distance from them.

Let us now ask the question: what is it assumed we know and value? What sense of the world is the text confirming for us? Well, it is assumed that we know that nothing in this world really matters much more than anything else, except it's better, if bullets are flying around, not to be on the receiving end. As we've seen from earlier talk in the movie, it's immaterial whether you're talking about what they call a quarterpounder with cheese in France or quoting the Bible. Both are equally meaningful or meaningless. The scene confirms that 'shit happens'. There is no way that we are positioned to believe that it was divine intervention. It's random: some people don't get shot, others do. We know it's funny if someone misreads the randomness as a reason for religious conversion, particularly if they articulate their vision liberally sprinkled with four-letter words. We know too that it's better not to have the emotions deeply engaged, but rather to live on the surface. Anything else is more than slightly ludicrous. Everything is literally a matter of life and death, but that's not very serious. In short, the text as a whole is, in many ways, the epitome of postmodern cool (see Grossberg, 1989 on postmodernism).

The actual experience the text gives us however is really very intense, because it depends on shock, and a quick succession of different reactions. When the fourth man bursts into the room, we expect a bloodbath (even though logically we know that Jules and Vincent don't get killed), but the text denies us that, substituting the comic shock of the miraculous deliverance. There is no violence seen – we don't even see the fourth man take the bullets – but then unexpectedly the pattern we expected is completed by the violence being displaced onto poor Marvin. Besides, there is something wildly transgressive going on. In the context of the rather ridiculous 'religious' discussion about divine intervention, and with its sheer unexpectedness, the shooting is undeniably comic, but we realise it's the kind of thing it's in bad taste to laugh at, and so the reaction transgresses standard codes of behaviour. It emotionally underlines that sense that things matter but they don't matter. Shit happens.

The film is playing around with genre too. As I've said, these are gunmen unlike other gunmen, but the film isn't a parody or a satire: rather it's taking the forms of the genre, providing a pastiche of them, playing with and subverting our generic expectations, so that the narrative thrills are there in a comic mode without the solemnity of classic crime fiction. Again, in terms of genre, we are positioned to appreciate the play quality, rather than commit ourselves to the values implicit in the classic form of it. It produces the 'blank irony' that Jameson sees as characteristic of the postmodern.

Asking questions about how we're positioned, and how the text plays on our desire for confirmation and our desire for intense experience, leads to making explicit the ideology of the text. You may not like it; you may think it's fine. The point is, once you've articulated how the text is asking you to see the world, the ideology is there for inspection.

I want to stress that I am not setting up a critique here of the values of *Pulp Fiction*. I am not suggesting for a minute that it is a pernicious text and students ought to be warned against the ideology it is promoting. (In fact, I think *Pulp Fiction* is a terrific film.) All that I am arguing for is that students need to be made aware

1 that it is a text, and that the world it creates is a product of textual strategies; and
2 that, however seductive a framework it provides for telling the story of our lives, it is only one of the many possible frames, and corresponds to only one of the many possible selves.

In other words, I want students to have the strategies to acknowledge the limits of the experience being offered, become fully engaged with it if that happens, but not to see it as the whole world. No-one can live their whole life as if it were *Pulp Fiction*, any more than they can live their whole life as if it were *Pride and Prejudice*. I suspect trying to live your life as if it were *Pride and Prejudice* would be a lot more dangerous and disabling these days than using *Pulp Fiction* as a frame: there are not many Mr Darcys around (although a lot of men who still subscribe to the patriarchal beliefs that are so thoroughly inscribed in the romantic ideology of the book). The kind of offhand scepticism promoted by *Pulp Fiction* may in the end be rather more healthy than that.

Pulp Fiction, as I said, is inevitably a tale told out of school. However, the work done on stories in school, stories like *Pride and Prejudice* perhaps, must be geared to equipping our students to deal with that story, and all the other stories that, in very profound ways, make up their lives.

References

Althusser, L. (1984) *Essays on Ideology*, London: Verso.

Austen, J. (1972) (1813) *Pride and Prejudice*, Harmondsworth: Penguin.

Beach, R. (1993) *A Teacher's Introduction to Reader-Response Theories*, Urbana: NCTE.

Belsey, C. (1980) *Critical Practice*, London: Methuen.

Cohan, S. and L. Shires (1988) *Telling Stories: A Theoretical Analysis of Narrative Fiction*, New York and London: Routledge.

Corcoran, B. and E. Evans, eds (1987) *Readers, Texts, Teachers*, Upper Montclair: Boynton/Cook.

Davies, B. (1993) *Shards of Glass: Children Reading and Writing Beyond Gendered Identities*, St Leonards: Allen & Unwin.

Davis, L. (1987) *Resisting Novels: Ideology and Fiction*, New York and London: Methuen.

Eliot, G. (1965) (1871–2) *Middlemarch*, Harmondsworth: Penguin.

Fairclough, N. (1992) *Discourse and Social Change*, Cambridge, Massachusetts: Polity Press.

Foucault, M. (1972) *The Archaeology of Knowledge*, London: Tavistock.

Freire, P. (1972) *Pedagogy of the Oppressed*, Harmondsworth: Penguin.

Freire, P. and D. Macedo (1987) *Literacy: Reading the Word and the World*, Massachusetts: Bergin and Garvey.

Freund, E. (1987) *The Return of the Reader: Reader-Response Criticism*, London: Methuen.

Gee, J. P. (1990) *Social Linguistics and Literacies: Ideology in Discourses*, London: Falmer Press.

—— (1992) *The Social Mind: Language, Ideology and Social Practice*, New York: Bergin and Garvey.

Gilbert, P. (1989) *Writing, Schooling and Deconstruction*, London: Routledge.

Gilbert, P. and S. Taylor (1991) *Fashioning the Feminine: Girls, Popular Culture and Schooling*, North Sydney: Allen & Unwin.

Grossberg, L. (1989) 'Pedagogy in the Present: Politics, Postmodernity, and the Popular' in *Popular Culture, Schooling and Everyday Life*, eds H. Giroux and R. Simon, Massachusetts: Bergin and Garvey.

Jameson, F. (1981) *The Political Unconscious: Narrative as a Socially Symbolic Act*, London: Methuen.

Lawson, H. (1986) (1892) 'The Drover's Wife', in *The Penguin Henry Lawson: Short Stories* ed. J. Barnes, Ringwood: Penguin.

Lemke, J. (1995) *Textual Politics: Discourse and Social Dynamics*, London: Taylor and Francis.

Misson, R. (1993a) 'MTV: Music, Textuality, Video', *English in Australia* (103): 4–13.

—— (1993b) '(Un)Popular Culture', *Viewpoint* 1(2): 3–4.

—— (1994a) 'Advertising Textuality', *Interpretations* 27(1): 16–27.

—— (1994b) 'Every Newsstand Has Them: Teaching Popular Teenage Magazines', in *Knowledge in the Making: Challenging the Text in the Classroom*, eds B. Corcoran, M. Hayhoe and G. Pradl, Portsmouth NH: Heinemann Boynton/Cook, 73–89.

—— (1994c) 'Making it Real, Making it Mine', in *Realising the Future*, AATE Conference Proceedings, Perth.

—— (1995) 'Living the Lifestyle: The Attractions of Seinfeld.' *Australian Journal of Comedy* 1(2): 55–75.

Silverman, K. (1983) *The Subject of Semiotics*, New York: Oxford University Press.

Tarantino, Q. (1994) *Pulp Fiction*, London: Faber and Faber.

Tompkins, J. P., ed. (1980) *Reader–Response Criticism: From Formalism to Post-Structuralism*, Baltimore and London: Johns Hopkins University Press.

Weedon, C. (1987) *Feminist Practice and Poststructuralist Theory*, Oxford: Basil Blackwell.

6

Old letteracy or new literacy

Reading and writing the wor(l)d online

Wendy Morgan

Introduction: mapping the terrain

Variously modulated across the chapters of this book is a concept of literacy as a social practice which, like its learning, is therefore always contingent on cultural and historical contexts and available technologies. This chapter also takes such a view of literacy – or more properly literacies – and explores the relationship of print-based, alphabetically encoded 'letteracy' to newer forms of electronically mediated literacy – the 'computency' (Green, 1988; Bigum and Green, 1993) which aligns competence in literacy with computers.

My exploration is grounded in a number of narratives drawn from a series of case studies of technologised literacy learning in three schools linked by a wide area network in the Atherton Tablelands. This high plateau lies in the hinterland of Cairns, a coastal town in far north Queensland; in the Coral Sea beyond is the Great Barrier Reef. The Tablelands comprise world heritage listed wet tropical rainforest, rich grazing land, lakes and rivers, stony ridges, dry scrub and little townships. Many of those far-flung towns have schools, some of them with only one or two teachers and a handful of students. But these isolated schools across 6,000 square kilometres, some of them designated disadvantaged through isolation and poverty, have since 1995 become linked electronically with one another and with people across the world through a wide area network called BushNet.[1]

It might seem that field work in so atypical an environment as the rural tropics of the Atherton Tablelands would yield very little that could be applied to other contexts. That is of course both a limitation of any case study and also its strength, in offering 'thick' descriptions (to use Geertz's famous term) of perhaps peculiar particulars and thus accounting more adequately for the phenomenon being considered. Without making a dubious move towards generalisation from limited instances that of their nature cannot be replicated, my arguments about these particulars may serve as propositions or hypotheses that invite exploring and modifying in other cases. Certainly the literacies described here prompt questions about changing contexts for changing practice in its local manifestations within an increasingly webbed world. If there are no prompt answers to these questions, no tidy conclusions and recommendations, that is more properly responsive in a multifarious and unstable world of textual practice.

Marginalising technologised literacy

Our first example is of a practice not directly observed but narrated to me by a Year 4 teacher (here called Betty) who described herself as having come to computers rather lately and rather reluctantly. Her classroom is a large colourful space with plenty of evidence of students' writing and drawing around the walls and with an old Mac classic off to one side, used for game playing as students complete their set tasks. Betty showed me a class book for which the students had contributed recounts of their recent camping trip to the far west of the state. Their word-processed texts had been glued onto big pages, illustrated by the students, and laminated.

Betty described the processes of this writing: first she helped edit the students' drafts and correct spelling, grammar and punctuation. When each piece was 'ready' the student writer took it to a teacher aide ensconced in a cubicle off a passageway beyond the classroom where a Macintosh 575 sat. Here the student keyed in the text under the aide's watchful eye and hand in managing files and discs. No further editing occurred in this process. When the child returned to the room a classmate was sent out to do likewise.

As Betty explained, she knew it was important that her students should become competent computer users: this has been her way of taking up the challenge. The teacher aide, who is more skilled with computers, is in control of the technology: the students do not control the management of files. Nor are the more experienced among them delegated responsibility as 'buddies' to work with their peers, for Betty would not have them miss out on important classroom work. Indeed, she deliberately located the computer beyond the classroom proper so that any student working on it would not be distracted by ongoing lesson activities.

While this very brief account of classroom computer use is only one, perhaps atypical, instance it may be useful to instantiate a number of points about literacy and technology as a practice with a number of dimensions which are changing, albeit unevenly, in an age fast becoming technologically saturated.

Literacy as a practice

A material practice

Literacy always involves a particular relationship between language and the available technologies for recording and communicating information.

It involves objects: we sit at desks, using books and computers; we may still use the old-fashioned technology of a pen. The material technologies affect how we read and write and what we take reading and writing to be. What was the 'natural' length of a document when it had to fit on an ancient Roman parchment roll? What is a letter, who is the author of a letter, and when is it signed off – when we can insert our own ideas into an e-mail from someone else and zap them straight back to the sender on the other side of the world at the speed of light, to await a similarly annotated return? The material technologies also affect us materially as readers and writers, from our posture at a keyboard staring at a screen to our sense of ourselves as intimately connected to those electronic prostheses that extend the reach of our senses and minds.

With the materiality of any literacy practice in mind, we return to Betty's classroom. Its distribution of spaces and determination of their functions locates the computer for 'serious' purposes out of the way of any uses integral to classroom activities. This declares to students that the technology has no central place in the culture of this micro-world.

For of course no technology can be merely material objects and artefacts: it cannot ultimately be separated from the social and cultural practices that grow up around it as we use it to our social and cultural purposes. (So too it shapes us.) Hence an always technologised literacy is . . .

An historical practice

It is a practice that develops in and for a specific time and place and changes over time. The machinery changes with the times too, and with this the practices and cultures around it. Readers as old as me may remember manual typewriters and carbon paper copies – and the slips of correction paper we slid between the copies to erase and over-type a mistake. As a research assistant in the 1970s I laboured for months to check and type out my employing professor's handwritten manuscript which dealt with Chaucer's handwritten poems (later printed and orthographically edited by generations of scholars working backwards to an unattainable correctness). Today of course such a scholar would have been conducting full word searches on digital manuscripts, establishing databases of citations and references, drafting, keying in and editing his own work almost simultaneously and far more expedititiously, and the research assistant would be otherwise employed – or unemployed.

As this example demonstrates, electronic technologies have made possible new kinds of texts which demand new literacy skills to manage them. These text types include information genres such as spreadsheets, databases, hypertextually linked web pages, e-mail discussion lists; multimedia genres which combine in new ways written text, visual images, animation, video, music and sound effects, real-time simulations, graphical displays and the like; and informal, immediate, global communications genres that allow us to share one to one, one to many, many to one via e-mail, web boards, IRCs and the like.

In Betty's classroom the capabilities of the computer have been harnessed to produce that older technology, the book; indeed, even the full editing potential of the word processor has not been utilised. As this volume bears witness, there is nothing wrong with book production in itself; but it would be a pity if those students did not come to understand how the historically once dominant technology of the codex or printed book has been supplemented and at times supplanted by other machines for the storing and retrieval of information and the telling of stories. (We shall shortly see another teacher in the same school pushing beyond the bounds of that older form.)

It will already be apparent that such historically contingent technologies and texts inevitably entail changes in our social and cultural practice too, for literacy *is* . . .

A social and cultural practice

A technology is a tool for any of a number of purposes, and is a means by which things get done socially and culturally. But a tool also shapes purposeful activities around it. As we have seen, a technology, or a tech-nologised literacy, also constitutes sociocultural institutions, practices and even people's sense of self and place and scope for action as members of a literate community. And while we may be at the centre of one community, with its particular stories about our cultural world and its peculiar ways of 'doing' reading and writing, we may be at the margin of another, with its different social and cultural practices of literacy. Which groups 'do' a computerised literacy most comfortably – as if they were born to it – in our society? Or do it in a way which is most rewarded? Which groups or individuals are systematically poor in access to information and to 'our' ways of doing things with symbols, because they're 'unwired'?

Consider Betty's classroom in the light of these questions. When her students are dismissed to solitary confinement under a teacher aide's surveillance to do their word processing, they may be learning where the letters are on a keyboard, but they aren't learning about the sociable nature of literacy. This not only involves us in face-to-face interactions with others around texts and screens; it entails also developing a sense of an audience for our writing and participation in an ongoing conversation or argument. While Betty's students are contributing to the shared stock of memories enshrined in the class book of their camp, their audience is more limited than if they were able to interact with others in an extended, potentially global community via the computer. And via the book any conversations are (literally) only one way.

In this and in other ways a technologised literacy is . . .

A political practice

It is involved with people's relative power, authority and status to mean and to act and to gain access to the world's goods and advantages. This point follows inevitably from the previous one – because where there are social and cultural communities, there will also be differences and discrepancies between communities, hence also inevitably inequalities and inequities. Those differences, and all that follows from them, involve literacy. Any text promotes or represents as commonsense, normal or desirable a particular culture's way of being in the world and acting on it. And any culture will promote or represent as commonsense, normal or desirable a particular way of being literate around texts. Particular kinds of (technologised) texts and textual practices may in gross or infinitely subtle ways affect the life chances of those who do not feel at home in the texts and practices of others who are culturally, economically and politically powerful in a society.

In Betty's classroom the political is of course threaded through all those other aspects of a technologised literacy. That is clear if we consider only the relationships of power between teachers and students: who is identified as the expert in those technologies of writing and computer use, and who is kept dependent on those experts in learning how to work on the raw material of experience. Consider who directs, and who is directed, who takes the initiative, and who follows. This is not to suggest that ignorance should flourish, nor that students can learn by osmosis, independently of explicit teaching, nor that Betty is simply a 'poor' teacher in maintaining these relations of dependence. Far from it: she teaches as best she can, in the way she knows best, and her teaching produces students with certain literate capacities which are honoured in her and her students' communities.

No practice is simply bad. Nor is any entirely innocent. There is a variety of sometimes complementary, sometimes discrepant ways of practising a technologised literacy. The rest of this chapter explores further examples – or rather, constructs exemplary stories – which of course are capable of other readings than those I offer. As well as tracing the dimensions identified above, in these instances I take up issues of an apprenticeship into these emergent forms and practices of literacy. What teaching practices induct students into which culture of technologised literacy? What might make them duly appreciative and properly critical of that culture?

A different practice for difference

Another Year 4 teacher (let's call him Ken) has recently held a teaching post at a small remote school in the far western outback of Queensland. His twelve students, all Aboriginal, had access to four computers, not yet linked to the Internet via BushNet. The school was also furnished with a huge library of more than 4,000 books – but the students could find almost none that were relevant to their experience in their environment and culture. In response, Ken came up with the same idea as Betty: to construct some class books in which his students could find themselves. But he took it a step further. What follows is his account, as he told it to me, while he showed me what they had created.

> My approach was based on the Aboriginal culture. I'd get the Aboriginal elders to come in and tell one of their traditional stories to the children, an Aboriginal teacher aide and myself. The two of us teachers would compare notes afterwards and write down the story. We'd then take it back to the elders and ask them if our version was what they'd been saying, and change it to whatever they wanted. Then the teacher aide and I would generate a sequence of rough sketches that represented the story, each on a piece of butcher's paper. Next I'd retell the story to the children, with the elders listening in. Sometimes we'd have got the elders to retell the story beforehand, then we'd retell it using the pictures. After that the children would generate written text relating to the pictures – generally one or two simple sentences relating to what we'd drawn. We'd then allocate a page, with its one or two sentences, to a child, who'd do an illustration for it. So then we'd have the illustrations, the text, we'd put the text onto card, and we'd sequence the pictures and the text, and so on. We'd do a whole heap of language activities based on that text – sequencing, cloze, word recognition for the Year Ones, grammar etcetera.
>
> Then I'd take a photograph of each picture in 35mm, take it through Photoshop, and drop it into Hypercard. And in Hypercard we'd key in the text, so the kids would have the story in English on Hypercard, with their pictures.
>
> The next step was to get the elders to come in and tell the story in their own Aboriginal language, and we'd record that on computer. The two people that speak in these electronic books can't read or write – one of them signs his name with an X. They'd never seen such books before, never even worked with text. We had to step our way through the story text so they could work out what they were going to say to each page to get the sequencing as per the written text.
>
> Before I left I was in the process of making them similar to those electronic 'living books'. Each of the stories has got the Aboriginal language version on it as well as English, and the intention was to put a button on each of the words so you could click on a word and it would replay the English word for you. But the translation is pretty approximate, because

of course it's not possible to do a direct translation word for word from the Aboriginal language to English or vice versa.

On my asking if Ken could give me a copy of these 'living books' he replied: 'No. Though I can share it with people on a professional level, the kids [in his present school] can't use it: I've made a real point with them that this is a possession of the Aboriginal community.'

One day [back in his previous school] we sat down in a language lesson round these books, and one of the kids said, 'Oh, this story here's just like the story in that book in our library.'

He went and got the book. We then read this Aboriginal story written by a white feller and the two elders. (I'd previously asked them, 'Can you just not say anything for a while?') When I finished reading I said to the kids, 'Where did this story come from?'

'This feller made it up' (pointing to the author's name).

'Where did he get it from?'

'He got it from his head.'

Well, the two elders were stunned to think the stories of their culture came from a white man's head – because there's absolutely no acknowledgement in any of the books to the local people.

So I've made a real point with each of these electronic books that their names are to it, and it's a possession of the Aboriginal community, not of the school. It's something that I've always pushed them on, that they have to keep ownership. When the white feller author saw some of these stories, he said to the elders, 'Would you like to come up and do a story with us?' And they said, 'No, we do it with the school now.' They realised what had been going on, because he's done very well out of their stories. One frustrating thing is: his stories aren't suitable for the Aboriginal classroom, because they're written by a white feller and the language in them is inappropriate for Aboriginal kids. I mean, the kids all speak English as a second language. But if you look at the language in these [electronic books], it's kid generated: that's the stuff that the kids know. We've edited the stories, but we've edited them very, very cautiously to make sure that we retain as much as we can for the kids but give it in Australian English, rather than Aboriginal English.

We had a National Aboriginal and Islander Day of Celebration about three weeks before I left. The whole Aboriginal community came in for it, and we put a computer out in the under-cover area. (The parents refuse to go into a classroom – they've got unhappy memories of school.) We had the computer running and there was always a crowd at it, watching and listening. They got a big kick out of it.

This narrative speaks largely for itself; and to draw out its implications by comparison with Betty's book manufacture may seem odious. You might say that she has taken as large a step from her known practices as he has. (Indeed, before Ken started this project he knew nothing about hypercard or multimedia applications; he learned as he went along in pursuing his goal of creating a culturally appropriate resource for his students that would combine the oral with the written with the visual.) The point is not to focus on Ken or Betty as worthy of blame or praise. They each have their competence; they have each been shaped by their particular history, experiences and culture, and they act according to their beliefs about how students should learn literacy and how electronic technologies can contribute to this. Instead let us explore for a moment the material, socio-cultural and political implications of this example of a technologised literacy practice.

It might seem that apart from the computer itself these electronic books are *im*-material: there are no literal traces for our senses to grasp in hard drive or disc. But of course there are very different material consequences for those Aboriginal people, depending on whether their stories, so inti-mately woven into and out of their land, remain in their community as a resource or are 'mined' and exported like minerals to profit someone else. Consider the culture and politics being played out in this classroom. The authorisation of the story rests with the elders; the teacher is learning from them, even as he uses his own expertise to capture their words. The students are learning to retell their community's stories, not someone else's. And they are also learning that a group like theirs can in partnership with others appropriate new technologies in order to both preserve and trans-form those stories for a culture which is also undergoing change.

Literacy and technology learning

At this point I want to return to those concepts about literacy and elec-tronic technologies outlined on pp. 130–3, and as promised overlay some points about learning. As my two vignettes suggest, any classroom is a mini-society, which suggests to students what it means to be a proper member of the classroom subculture and therefore how to behave in literate ways around computers.

In what follows I draw heavily on the work of Bigum and Green (1993) in describing three overlapping concepts relating to technology and literacy learning. These concepts are: the operational, the cultural and the critical.

The operational

This means learning language, or learning how to use the computer. It means getting to know what the computer does, or what letters do: how squiggles on a page or screen represent sounds, words, concepts. Beyond these beginnings it means (among many other things) learning when different registers are appropriate and how different kinds of texts are constructed generically and lexicogrammatically to do their characteristic work.

These basics are undoubtedly important; however, they are insufficient on their own. It would be a mistake – one often advocated by politicians, journalists and parents – to assume that this constitutes the beginning and end of literacy learning, and that students should move from the parts (letters to words to sentences to paragraphs to whole texts) in a rational seeming progression. The error lies in not understanding that the learning of these skills is much more properly – and readily – accomplished when it is richly contextualised by being embedded in the following:

The cultural

This means learning through language, and through technology. It means knowing what you can do with computers – or with a genre: how to utilise the technologies to your purposes, your ends. It means developing the skills for expert performance. It means learning through use – developing reading skills as you read a text for pleasure or information. This constitutes a kind of apprenticeship: learning on the job in carrying out the everyday practices of the 'workshop' – the textshop (Ulmer, 1985), the computer interface. Students in this realm are far more competent than those who are only in the operational sphere, having been acculturated to the technologies and their attendant literacies. But that very immersion is wanting, perhaps even hazardous, if unaccompanied by the third component:

The critical

This entails understanding what computers, and language, can do with people to shape their forms of living and their life chances. It means grasping something of the material, historical, social, cultural and political dimensions of technological and literacy practices mentioned above. Such evaluation eventually involves, I believe, an ethical responsibility to foster practices that are likely to benefit society as a whole rather than furthering the economic and political advantage of a minority.

As outlined above this triad carries all the risks of its neatness. In practice these aspects are likely to be dynamic: overlapping, interweaving. The next section attempts to convey something of this necessary complication in describing another classroom, to explore this idea further, that being literate and 'computent' means entering into the cultures of literacy and computing.

Solar tracks across the centre of Australia

In another classroom in the same school where Ken teaches we look at how online technology is being utilised to integrate various curriculum activities in maths, geography and English. This is a multi-age class (Years 4. 5 and 6) in an old wooden block. (During World War II the school was used as a military headquarters and hospital – and morgue – for American troops engaged in the battle of the Coral Sea.) The classroom has somewhat battered cream walls and a clean but tired brown carpet. An adjoining room gives them extra space, and in that is a computer with CD-ROM and Internet link. The computer actually belongs to the Aboriginal Student Support and Parent Awareness Committee. Since the school could not furnish a computer for her room, the teacher, Heather Greder, made an arrangement with the Aboriginal community: her class has the use of the computer on condition that whenever members of the community want to use it, they have prior right, in or out of school time. In return for her students' access, Heather has been helping them get up their web page, scan in their paintings and the like.

The season is early summer and the time, before morning school. Already the ceiling fans are on high, stirring the steamy air. A number of children – Aboriginal, Caucasian – are socialising with their teacher and one another. In the adjoining room two Year 6 students have logged on to the web and accessed the site for a solar-powered car race, at that time in progress from Darwin to Adelaide across the desert heart of Australia. The two are checking the progress of the cars with keen interest because they've entered a contest and hope to win the $300 prize to put towards the class computer fund. (They had to estimate the arrival time of the first three place getters – and incidentally learned quite a lot about averages as they managed the complicated calculations.) The web site tells them that the first cars have got to a certain checkpoint; but there's no map on the site to show where that place is. (Later that morning, the Year 6 students would pull out the older technology of an atlas and track it down: a cattle station just over the border in South Australia.)

In following the leaders the students are participating doubly in a culture of competition – the race, and their contest. Moreover, not only is the information accessed technologically, it is also about a technological phenomenon. What lesson might the students be learning unconsciously by means of this 'teaching technology'? – among other things, perhaps, that up-to-date, immediately accessible facts are valuable in an information economy. That the latest technologies (solar cars, the web) are worth attention and celebration. That the kind of data that matter in this case concern car specifications, average kilometers per hour and so on. That speed is unquestionably praiseworthy. In such ways these students are being apprenticed to a technologised culture, and they are certainly eager participants: keen to win, keen to check how their calculations measure up to the 'reality' they know only by this and other forms of electronic mediation.

There is no suggestion here of a sinister plot to brainwash these innocents.

But as suggested earlier, all texts (like this solar car race site) and all technologies are inevitably caught up in promoting certain values, certain politics. So how would a critical literacy practice engage with this technologised text?[2] It might mean the teacher just musing aloud about that mania for 'winning', conceived in a certain way. It might mean the class taking a reverse direction at the same time, following a nineteenth-century abortive expedition by Burke and Wills as they trekked north from Melbourne toward the Gulf of Carpentaria. It might mean considering the tragic irony of that older expedition: those explorers were so proudly one-eyed about their white feller technologies – camping gear and rifles, maps and compasses – that they couldn't recognise that there was food and drink around them – which the Aborigines could have helped them find through *their* science and technology. The 'moral' of all this isn't that our present technologies are vastly superior to those of the industrialised Victorians; therefore our imagined teacher might be wondering why people think speed is so important, and what one might miss about the landscape by racing through it. And how one can know a land by traversing it in different ways – some of which are more invasive than others.

To complement this sketch of students engaging with a ready-made electronic document, the following episode, from the afternoon of that day, shows the class preparing to publish on the web. A computing enthusiast (Sarah Clutterbuck) who sometimes team-teaches with Heather is revising with the Year 6 students the hypertext markup language (html) tags for the home page each is preparing. She uses chalk on blackboard and the students copy them down on paper as she talks through with the class the logic of the codes. Her enthusiasm is infectious: all are attentive and several students plead with her ('Please!') when she offers to teach them some new codes, e.g. how to put in background colour. She tells them only about white; for other colours Sarah shows them how to search for themselves, going to View then to Source in existing web pages. She goes on to teach them how to size images to incorporate. (While Sarah is chalking up the tags, three students with literacy difficulties are working on the verandah with the learning support teacher, Robyn. They are labouring to write with pencil on paper self-descriptions for their web pages. 'My name is Larry and I am 12 years old . . . ' one writes with tedious difficulty and massive support from the teacher.)

The reason for this talk and chalk step in the process of home page construction is that the primary school does not have a lab of internet-worked computers. The lab at the neighbouring secondary school has been booked for a future evening to enable the students to get up their pages: they will involve their parents in typing in copy and will instruct them in inserting the tags. Heather is making a virtue of this necessity here – enrolling the parents as helpers in what she couldn't manage alone.

It is easy to identify the ironies in this vignette of students' learning to use a programming language (a metalanguage). Because the teachers and students have limited access to networked computers, the old literacy technologies (chalk, pencils) here persist as the means of instruction in the new. That is, the students are still 'doing it by the book' – writing instructions on paper for writing instructions for the computer. They are thus at this stage doubly dependent on the authority of the teacher's written word. Especially in these circumstances it is commendable that the learners are being given the means to become more independent by being shown how to discover the codes for themselves. (But theirs is a double advantage over those students with literacy difficulties, who are – necessarily? – excluded.)

Meanwhile, back in the desert the cars power on. Next day, the race is over. Before school, two girls are searching the web site for the winners' times, to check how close their calculations were. But – the unofficial results haven't been updated since yesterday, and the official results link ends in a blank page. Heather suggests that one of the girls, Breanna, could either phone the manager of the web page or e-mail him at the address given. Seeming pretty matter of fact about it, Breanna decides to write, and with Heather's help fixes on a subject title that will catch his attention: 'Anxious student'. Typing rather laboriously with two fingers of each hand, she composes the following, without help. (She rehearses a phrase or two aloud before keying it in or when part way through a sentence.)

Dear Mr Silver,

My name is Breanna Bailey. I'm a student at [. . .] State School. My class is a multi-aged class with Years 4, 5 and 6. We have entered your solar race competition. I was trying to find the first three place getters and the first car's arrival time but I couldn't find the results on the web site. Could you help us find the page with the results on it or could you e-mail us with the results. My address is . . .

Thank you
Breanna

This is an interesting snapshot of a literacy practice in a changing world. It's a social practice – a communication with an unknown adult beyond the classroom walls. Breanna takes this in her stride (despite being only eleven). And it's a cultural practice: she knows the genre of a formal letter to a stranger (although of course in other circumstances the immediacy of e-mail is changing the genre to something more informal, closer to talk). Breanna is learning how to take her place in this wider society with its technocultural ways of getting things done with words and data. She's becoming a member of a community of practice around technology and literacy – and this is also a matter of politics. Consider the power this child has relative to adults: the technology does have the effect of flattening out some hierarchies by providing easier access to those at the top. And consider the power this child has relative to her peers who aren't being so apprenticed to this practice.

It would be tempting to end on so resolutely clear a note. However, at the beginning of this section I promised complexities. So let us follow Breanna back into the main classroom, where Heather is reading aloud from *Sophie's World* by Jostein Gaarder. This is a challenging novel for adults, combining as it does a mystery story with 'an extraordinary tour through the history of Western philosophy' (as the jacket puts it) as the 'enigmatic' philosopher Knox undertakes the education of a fourteen-year-old Sophie. Heather is feeding it to the class in digestible mouthfuls and setting the students to write their thoughts in response to selected statements. Breanna is just in time to hear a philosopher warning about the limits of our knowledge and proposing a becoming humility as the proper response, rather than an arrogant or confident expectation that all information is our right.

There's a piquant contrast here. On the one hand (the race results) is knowledge presented as facts external to oneself but always accessible through the technologies. On the other (in the view of the philosopher) wisdom is presented as an internalised belief in the boundaries of our understanding. (This philosophy is a kind of moral technology, in that its practice works to shape people's subjectivities.) Such divergences – not of course articulated as such – have to be negotiated by the students through their literacy practices in this classroom. This is far from being a bad thing, provided that the education of these students continues to provide both the richness of such acculturation and the critical faculties to compare and evaluate the competing ideologies.

(Incidentally, in a later e-mail, Heather noted that one of the students *had* won the solar car competition. 'After consultation with the Deputy, he agreed to buy computer software and technology equipment for the school with *his* prize. . . . The class learned a hard lesson about competition versus cooperation, and the realities of student empowerment in a hierarchical system.')

Etracks – 'Showing where the people have been'

An increasing number of teachers are making use of the Internet to enable their students to access information and participate in 'ready made' projects like the solar car challenge. Fewer teachers I think are producing 'home grown' projects – though these do have advantages for their students. This next literacy event focusses on one such do-it-yourself project at another state primary school which is part of the network. This project is called 'Etracks' – electronic tracks; its logo is 'showing where the people have been' and its rationale is that 'communicating globally empowers a community locally'. The significance of this would not be lost on locals, for despite the sparkling new buildings which house the school the community has suffered economically in recent years, with the closure of railways, tin mining and forestry industries; the breadwinners of many families must commute to nearby towns for work.

Etracks was the brain child of Jerry Jeffress, one of the original BushNet organisers, and his wife Melissa. They had got interested in the possibilities of a global collaborative learning project, and the local school provided funding for them to work on the project part time. According to Jerry, the point of Etracks is not only to show students that this kind of communication and collaboration is possible but that 'it's essentially an ordinary thing; it's something that's no different than driving to town or to working as a timber cutter'. So a group of students at the school, from Years 3 to 7, are linked up with other students in Canada, Norway (at a similarly isolated small school on a small island), and New Zealand. They work together on projects and exchange information about the features of the topic – in this instance, endangered species – which are salient in their locality.

All the Etracks material – including messages between teachers and students – is archived at the site, because Jerry wanted this developing project to be open for anyone to read and trace its processes as well as products, failures as well as successes. (The capacity of the technology to capture conversational and epistolary exchanges means that it is much easier to present such 'audit trails' where the creators of a web site choose to present the ongoing processes of thinking and development. Where the will is there, this electronic literacy practice facilitates a social and political shift towards transparency – away from the norms of print publications which customarily conceal their sometimes errant steps along the way.)

The very public nature of Etracks has had several consequences. One concerns matters of content in the students' communications. Jerry has reminded the students of the difference between private messages and public communication by telling them that since everyone could read what they wrote, they shouldn't put up anything they wouldn't feel happy to see on a church bulletin board. Another consequence has to do with the formality or informality of the students' communication. When this project was first developed, teachers wanted to check the grammar and spelling of any e-mail messages. But Jerry thinks e-mail is like a casual conversation; he didn't want to be a 'grammar cop'. The school principal agreed with him, and the following advice now appears on the Etracks page: 'E-mail to the Etracks discussion list does NOT need to be run through a spell-checker before it gets sent. Focusing on the content of communication exchanged between primary students, we follow the philosophy of Sun Microsystems' Chief Executive Officer Scott McNealy: the content of e-mail is more important than perfect spelling and fancy formatting.' The same view prevails when the students are on the MOO. It's a different matter, however, when it comes to the students' web pages.

The Etracks page takes this position: 'Since we feel that web pages represent a (slightly) more permanent and formal presentation than e-mail, the Australian students' web pages for Etracks are being edited and corrected in line with accepted regional practice.'

These various forms of electronic exchange have a common theme – as mentioned, endangered species. One of the collaborative projects involves e-mail interviews between students across the globe, which are then formatted for the web. In another activity, the students are carrying out their own investigations into animals at risk of extinction. For example, at this school a couple of students have conducted a face-to-face interview with a local naturalist, and with help from Melissa and Jerry have edited it, marked it up and published their report on the web. Further reports are to follow by other participants. In addition, students will meet online in a MOO for real-time interaction, to discuss their projects and get to know one another.

Consider the operational and cultural aspects of electronic literacy involved in those investigations. A range of literacy skills is being practised here: planning for and conducting the interview; writing up and editing the text; and learning the html tags in order to publish it on the web. In this range of processes these students are acquiring a sense of what it means to be literate in an electronic environment. Among other things it means using a browser to look at html source files; knowing how to make links; and knowing how to capture images on web pages. As Jerry remarks, these are meta-skills, meta-knowledge about literacy: not visible in the final product as presented to the world, but essential to support the development of that product.

Consider too the community of practice involved in this 'home made' project. If you compare it with the solar car challenge, you can see that Etracks gives the students more scope to bring their own texts to the centre rather than being marginal to someone else's scene. At present of course the purposes and concerns of Etracks originate with the teachers. So the community is perhaps a little contrived – though no more so than most other school endeavours. Of course these are very young apprentices within this electronic culture. It may be that in time, out of this flow of communication across the globe, the students might exercise more initiative and make pathways that follow their own interests. Meanwhile what we see here may be a first step in a demonstration that (in the words of the Etracks logo) 'communicating globally empowers a community locally'.

But if that local empowerment is to happen it may be necessary to provide a critical context for the use of the technologies. It could mean teachers prompting students to ask, among other things, how it has come to be that these species are endangered. Whose technology and economics have driven these creatures to the margins of extinction? What are the politics of protesting about this situation: who doesn't want to know about it, and how can one spread the news among responsible people? How could communication and information technologies enhance and extend that spread? What action can be taken by young people as well as adults? And could there be power in knowledge: in realising that students across the globe are concerned about a crisis that involves us all, in our different ways? For teachers and students to seek answers to these questions might be to put the technologies to the service of a critical electronic literacy.

SuccessMaker: lessons in literacy

Retreating a little from this hope-filled vision, I now want to look by contrast at a different computer program at another school. This sets up a very different practice from Etracks – although, as its name makes clear, it claims that the students who use it are equally to be 'made' successful at school. This is an American program called SuccessMaker, which has a series of 'tutorials' in carefully graded levels, from preschool through senior secondary and adult education, in English, mathematics, language, science, life skills and other areas.

The school is currently conducting a trial of the program, which is to involve all the Year 8 and many of the Year 9 students. Apart from its more general applications, the staff see a particular advantage for their Aboriginal and Torres Strait Islander students, a number of whom have very delayed literacy development and need dedicated help – beyond what their classroom teachers can provide, for all their commitment – in 'getting up to speed' in literacy.

To give you some idea of how it works, let me share with you my impressions from the notes I made on my first encounter. (Of course, this constitutes my inevitably peculiar reading, from the position of an adult and a teacher educator who is clearly opinionated about preferable approaches to early literacy.)

> Menu: a number of workshops. I choose 'Reader's Workshop'. Isolated sentences, illustrated, with no context or explanation: e.g. 'Alex did not know where he was. Alex was . . . ' This is followed by multiple choices, including 'lost'. I hit this and the next screen comes up. 'Ann burned her hand on the pan.' What? How did we get from Alex to Ann? I'm the one that's lost! How could I make sense of this if I can't already read a series of words out of any context that would make them meaningful?
> . . . I try typing in the wrong answer, to be told: 'Try again.' When I select the right answer I get a winner's rosette and can go on to the next screen. Out of the blue, the screen delivers a poem about a boy getting his hair cut, followed by 'This writing is an example of a / poem / chapter / myth / tall tale.' Now, if I don't already know what a tall tale is – or a poem in this written, rhymed form, I'm stuck. And in any case, why should my attention be directed first to these pretty dubious cate-

gories? – After all, myths and tall tales can be in verse form. The next screen asks me to choose the best title for the poem. I'm offered choices like 'Paul's Haircut'; 'Paul is Afraid'. I choose the latter; I'm told, in firm, no nonsense print: 'This poem is about Paul's haircut.' I'm getting pretty dispirited by now.

So I exit and try another workshop with the more intriguing title of 'Reading Investigations'. Here we go: more of the same – 'My Japanese grandmothers were taught to walk with . . . steps: / enormous / dainty / sluggish / boisterous.' The picture shows a red headed female detective in a belted raincoat near a window showing a city nightscape. Is this multiculturalism, or rather cultural stereotyping? My steps to literacy are getting pretty sluggish wading through this stuff. The very next task is 'Complete the Analogy'. I'm nowhere told what an analogy is. 'Bored : . . . ; tired : energetic'. That's me: tired and bored.

As I said, this is my reading of my reading, which itself was a whistle stop tour – an attempt to get the flavour of the various workshops and some sense of their model of literacy learning. When I shared these notes with the school's computing studies teacher – let's call him Brian – who's a judiciously enthusiastic advocate of SuccessMaker, he commented, 'the students that are using SuccessMaker do not appear to be as dispirited as you. My experience is that the students do not get tired and bored using this program. Perhaps it's because they have been enrolled at the correct level and have worked through the previous sequential lessons at a pace that is commensurate with their needs. Students do not randomly flip through various levels of different courses.'

I try another workshop – 'Reading Adventures'. On the first page I'm told it's from 'My Friend Leslie: The Story of a Handicapped Child', by Maxine Rosenberg. It consists of less than a screen of text – I have no idea which part of the story it's from – and then the instruction 'Word Builder. Mark the word in the paragraph that has the same meaning as the highlighted word.' I do so and am told 'Nice work' and I'm given the sentence back reformulated, 'C's mother says J doesn't mean to bother, or annoy, C.' This is presumably designed to reinforce my learning. But what am I being taught about reading stories – except that it's about hunting for right answers to questions that may be irrelevant to my concerns? I'm certainly not being helped to learn about the satisfactions of following characters through the turns of a story line. Next screen – and the story's gone (it was just an exercise for drill, after all) – 'The mountain snows melted in the spring. Waterfalls began to pour off the edges of the / rivers / cliffs / clouds.' This, in the tropics of Australia! I rest my damp brow in my humid hand. I throw in the towel.

Now, this program claims to teach reading, but from my brief acquaintance

I believe it rather tests it, and could also teach teachers and students a very limited idea of what reading involves – even if there is an accompanying series of 'complete' books from which such extracts as I have just quoted are drawn.

But what was the view of the teachers who were testing the program? The learning support teacher shared with me her reservations, which turned out to be rather like mine, although according to Brian's testimony the previous learning support teacher (from 1992 to 1995) believed that the introduction of SuccessMaker was in part responsible for the greatest improvement in the Aboriginal students' literacy skills she had seen in her four years at the school. Brian also acknowledged her outstanding dedication and hard work in helping those students, and this is a useful reminder of the importance of the teaching context and uses of any technology; of itself no program can be wholly good or bad, and even the more fragmentary and brainless of drilling exercises could be rendered pretty innocuous if embedded in skilled and more enlightened teaching. However, I would also claim that such tutorial programs, founded as they are on certain assumptions about literacy learning, encourage the kind of transmissive teaching that is congruent with them.

Brian's expertise lies in teaching the use of computers, and he makes no claim to specialist knowledge in developing the literacy skills of students, particularly of those with difficulties. But in the less-than-ideal world of schools, he believes that SuccessMaker does many things right in helping such students:

1 In a classroom where some students have very low literacy, a teacher couldn't provide the material and the individual instruction which this program does.
2 It initially tests the students, then enrols them 'at the correct level' for their skill or knowledge.
3 It covers the range of skills and knowledge, such as vocabulary, at the level and at the rate of progress that suits each student.
4 It tutors the student on a one-to-one basis. If they have problems it gives them clues and prompts them before it comes up with the answer.
5 It gives constant reinforcement for the right answer.

Therefore, on balance, Brian judges that it makes a valuable contribution –

as an additional tool in the overall school approach to assist students in developing their literacy and numeracy skills. The actual amount of time spent on SuccessMaker per week, one to three periods out of thirty-five periods, represents only a very small fraction of their overall school week and there are many other strategies being employed in addition, to ensure a broad approach to assisting these students. In general I believe that the advantages outweigh the disadvantages:

students enjoy using the program and appear to make steady gains if they have sufficient access to SuccessMaker system, although, in a school situation where there are many strategies that are being employed it is not possible to clearly identify the amount of gain made by any one particular strategy.

However, Brian is also aware of its present shortcomings – such as the Americanisation of many topics and approaches and their irrelevance to Australian children, particularly to Aboriginal and Torres Strait Islander students. But he pointed out to me that the supplier of the program is likely to be involved in the gradual rewriting of many of the courses to include Australian content hence also perhaps the practices around it. Here lies an opportunity for teachers such as Brian, through the school's trialling, to contribute feedback and so help reshape some aspects of the technology. Brian would like to think that in the future 'we can include content that is especially targeted at Aboriginal students'.

Now it is doubtless true enough, that SuccessMaker can be a useful resource and supplementary tool for busy teachers – at least perhaps in that sphere of the operational mentioned earlier. But any computer technology is never just a resource, a tool – it also brings with it a context for learning and a culture for understanding (in this case) what you do to be a learner, and what counts as reading. So whatever answers the program gives students I think it leaves unanswered a number of more important questions – which would have to be supplied by informed teachers.

What does it mean to read successfully? How can we teachers, who understand the purposes of reading, who have been inducted into the culture and the practices of a reading community – how can we set up this kind of purposeful context for youngsters? Where is the scope for pleasure, for play and inventiveness, for imagination and for exploration? (The only fun I could detect that SuccessMaker offers students is in getting answers right and comparing their score with their previous performance.) Where are opportunities for judgment and critique? Or for using texts for one's own purposes?

This is the opinion of a very critical reader, on very brief acquaintance, and there will continue to be debates with and among those like the education department of Queensland and schools in other states of Australia and elsewhere that have invested their funds, hopes and beliefs heavily in SuccessMaker.

Research, of course, can be used to support or critique just about any teaching technology, and some such research – far more elaborate than the brief foray reported on here – supports the effectiveness of this program.[3] Such debates must be engaged if technology is to be used as wisely as possible for literacy.

But what of student users of SuccessMaker? Here is a little of what I saw and heard from some ATSI students who were 'enrolled'. Joe has been at the school for only a term; he's a virtually illiterate Year 8 Aboriginal boy, tall, with the gangliness of a young adolescent. In a learning support session he's sitting at a computer with earphones on, working his way through exercises from an 'Initial Reader' workshop: 'Word Meaning and Reading Sentences'. He laughs aloud when he answers correctly and a yellow rosette becomes an animated figure jumping for joy. At the end of the lesson his teacher checks his score with him: 77 per cent right: he has answered twenty-seven questions correctly . . .

Like Joe, Margaret came to the school in Year 7 from the Torres Strait. She speaks English as her second language and could not read when she was in Year 6. She's been using SuccessMaker consistently for a year. I asked her to describe what she did in reading at the computer:

Margaret: Fill in the missing answers and that.
              [This is SuccessMaker's definition of reading – like that of a number of teachers.]
Wendy: What's the best thing about SuccessMaker, as far as you're concerned?
Margaret: When you're getting it all right, all these little pictures coming out at you . . . . Sometimes I can beat my lower scores, like I'm going up.
Wendy: What's the worst thing about SuccessMaker?
Margaret: When I get it wrong.

(It seems that for this student the program is beyond criticism; she accepts its judgment of her errors.) Brian added to this fragmentary picture by noting that the school had recently conducted a survey/interview of about twenty-nine students who were using SuccessMaker: 'The overwhelming majority enjoyed using SuccessMaker, thought it helped them to learn, liked the way it would prompt and guide them if they were unsure of an answer and the way they could learn at their own pace.' None the less, I admit to some continuing concern that these youngsters like Joe and Margaret who come from richly oral and visual and contextually grounded cultures are being subjected (even for part of their schooling) to a program whose instruction in literacy is so narrow.

I think it would be a misguided hope that this technology will bring students like these in to the centre of a reading culture. In my more pessimistic moments I think that – especially if relied on almost exclusively – it would be the very thing that would keep such students as outsiders: as those who can only 'read by numbers', who won't be reading 'like a native' – that is, as natives who have inherited the realm of literacy and live comfortably in it as their own.

Home is where the page is

As we have seen already in sampling some of the uses of an online literacy in the BushNet schools, home pages are often the form in which students advertise their presence electronically. In this next section we consider for a little the issues of (schooled) identity to which this practice gives rise, by means of a snapshot of students who are geographically isolated making a small contribution to the global culture of the web via their home pages.

Currently a home page is a rather interesting case of an emerging genre, a new practice of literacy. In a transitional stage like this we're bound to get some examples that hark back to older, print forms, while others are more experimental – testing the potential of hypertext links, graphics, animation and sound – and therefore presenting an electronic version of the 'home owner' to be read potentially by that most unknown of public audiences, the millions of people world wide on the web.

It can sometimes be illuminating to read a school's web pages from both sides. We're mostly on the receiving side, consuming the product. This might enable us to read a little between the lines about the school: to infer something about the teaching contexts, the views of learning and technology that lead to this kind of product. But it is of course far more revealing if we're present to observe the other side: the process of production.

When the computing studies students at one of the high schools were first learning the technical aspects of how to produce web pages they were given a sheet of prompts that their teacher had adapted from a letter of introduction proforma. This includes the usual data: name, age, physical details, likes in music, hobbies, sports, family, friends, home and so on.

While some more confident students have diverged from this formula, a number of students have adhered to it in writing their self-descriptions; for while it offers a tried and true (maybe even a little tired) set of identifying characteristics, this structure, as Brian noted, 'has enabled them to construct a home page of which they are usually quite proud'; some would otherwise have been 'struggling for weeks'. And of course, one of the advantages of electronic publication is that the students can at any time during their years at the school refine and add to their home pages: their self-representations can be as volatile (or as stable) as themselves.

On the matter of the informational genre of the home page, Brian notes that many teachers of computing come from backgrounds in technical studies, science or mathematics. They may therefore have limited knowledge about and few strategies for developing students' literacy capacities for such writing – but in most cases would be open to constructive ideas about constructing the text of home pages. Brian is a case in point: having been alerted to this through my comments, he intends to encourage his students to create more individualised work in representing themselves in this medium.

Since most of these secondary students have utilised these prompts for their written text, during the few lessons of my observations many of them were busily engaged in choosing background 'wallpaper', importing a graphic they'd found and downloaded from the net or a photo they'd scanned. Regrettably, it's been no part of the brief of an English teacher to provide a structured approach to instruction in the aesthetic and practical principles of design and layout involving print and graphics. As part of the 'new literacy' skills the technology entails, they may need to take on aspects of what Brian includes in the two years of his computing studies course: desktop publishing and layout principles such as use of white space, direction, emphasis, suitability, opposition, balance, and cohesion. In the lessons I attended, Brian showed many of the students how to obtain a graphic from the screen by taking a print screen and inserting it in the LView-Pro graphics program, cropping it to size, saving it as a .gif file, making the background transparent and inserting it into their web page. These are very worthy skills for students to be developing, and some learn so fast they leave their teachers behind, especially where teachers provide them with the opportunity to do so. (Philip, for example has taught himself – with help – to include sound and moving graphics on his home page; see below.) Since in our multimedia environment such matters of visual re-presentation have increasing significance, there is an important opportunity here for teachers from a range of subject disciplines to work together on such production – as well as analysis and critique – of multimedia products with their students.

Let's look into a Year 9 computing studies lesson. One student – let's call her Alice – wants to substitute a new background for her home page, because 'I'm an individual', as she comments to Brian and the room at large while importing one from a collection of patterns on the web. Despite Brian's advice that a background should be just that, Alice chooses a highly assertive design – a solid red and green pattern of realistic apples – that makes her text illegible. This is her way of electronically representing her personality, her 'individuality', as she conceives of it: by these graphics rather than exclusively by the form of her writing.

In the home pages of Alice and her classmates is an instance of a 'hybrid' genre: a newer literacy practice just emerging from older ways of describing oneself and linking up with others. And if 'the style is the man', so too these students in creating such electronic multimedia representations of themselves are also 'hybrids' – young people on the threshold of a hypermediated environment; young people with a developing sense of their images, themselves, being disseminated globally. We do not yet know how this will alter their sense of self, their electronic subjectivity, as digital self-composition becomes more widely available and more complex in its forms. Perhaps much will depend on what regulation and surveillance – as well as opportunity – are provided within schools.

This chapter has offered a number of examples of practices in transition, and of tensions and contradictions between the old and the new, in texts and in classrooms and in conceptions of literacy. This kind of unevenness is almost inevitable in schools where teachers are making it up as they go along, on the basis of their past conceptions of literacy learning. Some of these they may seek to replicate even in new contexts; others they may be inventing beyond what their past knowledge has provided them with. As Brian commented, 'At many times one must take on the role of a fellow learner with the students and also be prepared to learn from the students.'

Learning the ABC of a technologised literacy

Brian's last-quoted comment suggests that if teachers (among whom I include myself) are to move further along the path towards a technologically textured future, we need to consider not just literacy practices but also learning practices. How can we set up a learning community for a culture of learning that is appropriate to the experiences and understandings of students who increasingly inhabit a hypermedia environment?

We shall not return to Betty and Ken, Heather and Brian, Melissa and Jerry to trace their theories in action. Instead, to begin to answer that question we listen to what a couple of Year 10 boys at the secondary school have to say about learning and computers.

Philip and Jacob are two of Brian's computer systems administrators (who include also girls); they help the other students to maintain their web pages and put up contributions to the student online magazine. The sharpness of their insights into learning is illuminating – and a reminder that we teachers need to listen more carefully than we perhaps do to what our students have to say on the subject. The boys' comments I believe apply to literacy learning even though they were talking mostly about learning technology and learning through technology.

For example, the boys and I were talking about how the other students were somewhat dependent on their teacher to talk them through various operations on the computer:

Jacob: They'll be able to tell you that they clicked this button and it happened, but they won't be able to tell you why that happened. That's like you're getting there but not understanding how you're getting there.

Wendy: Mmm. That kind of understanding I think is pretty important, and you people obviously do, too.

Philip: Yes. It's like the alphabet. Anyone can say the alphabet.

Jacob: But do you understand how to formulate the alphabet, make it make sense? . . .

[Such a nice way of putting what's sometimes called 'computer literacy'.] The two went on to explain what they learned from exploring computer applications:

Philip: You think methodically about the computer, and if you're with the computer all the time, you automatically start thinking methodically [about maths].

Jacob: And you start to understand it and think about it as a tool, as an extension, instead of as a big mystery, so you can start to use it for more things . . .

So too literacy can become a tool rather than a mystery. But as I've suggested, tools are never merely that – they involve social practices that also shape the tool makers. This becomes clear in the boys' next comments, which indicate how much they are at home in the realm of the cultural – of learning through computers, of doing things with them.

Wendy: You boys would have learnt that more or less by experimenting, by playing around, trying out, that kind of thing?

Philip: And working with Mr P and Mr T.

Jacob: Yes. See, we did computer studies, we did learn things like spreadsheets and all that, but then lunch times, before school and that, when you're just experimenting, and you go – 'Mr T, what's this doing? How do we get into there? How do we find that?' And so it's like exploring on your own, but with someone there to get you past the hard bits.

Wendy: That's right. Otherwise you're just sort of fearful in case it happens again?

Jacob: Or you're not going to be as careful next time. If you're just told this is going to happen, the borders of reason aren't going to be as clear . . .

Here are surely words that apply to learning more generally – as 'exploring on your own, but with someone there to get you past the hard bits'; and as getting to know where 'the borders of reason' lie – the limits of any system or field of knowledge or form of meaning making. In exploring those borders, Philip and Jacob are finding their way into the centre of a techno-logical culture. Listen to them describing what I'm calling an apprenticeship (that is, learning as you go, participating in practice with the help of skilled guides, in situations which approximate to those that pertain outside formal schooling). Consider the implications for the learning we set up in our class-rooms:

Jacob: Say if we're doing a spreadsheet, people are going to complain, 'Oh, it's boring, we've got spreadsheets again,' because all they're doing is exactly what Mr P is saying: 'Click this button here, click this button there, and this will happen.' And they're not actually going ' . . . And I wonder what this button over here does?' – they're just doing exactly what he says, and then that's it. You know, you've got to be able to press this button over here and then check what this one over there does.

Philip: You don't really need a lot of experience; you just need to be inquisitive, really, to find the things out. . . . You start experimenting with things, and when you can make things happen, you feel as though you've got power and you can make things happen, so you start exploring more . . .

In comments like these Philip and Jacob indicate how literacy today, as always, involves material technologies; how it is social and cultural and political in its practices and consequences. They have traced the three overlapping dimensions – the operational, the cultural and the critical – that are involved in a community of practice to which they are already apprenticed. That last dimension has been somewhat underplayed in most of the episodes glimpsed in this chapter – but the politics of a technological literacy most certainly need to be there in teachers' minds and teaching practice if the culture to which we are apprenticing students is to supplement older forms of 'letteracy' with emerging kinds of hypermediated literacy.

Notes

1   These cases are among a number of school-based studies which form part of an Australian Language and Literacy Policy Project funded by the Department of Education, Employment, Training and Youth Affairs. The project has conducted research into current practices and future directions in technology and language and literacy learning in primary and secondary schools, as these are framed by current theories about literacy and technology and shaped by national and state educational policies. See Bigum, Lankshear *et al.* 1977.

2   I define critical literacy in the following way in Morgan 1997: 1–2:

Critical theories of literacy derive from critical social theory and its interest in matters of class, gender and ethnicity. Both share the view that society is in a constant state of conflict, for the possession of knowledge (hence power), status and material resources is always open to contest. Struggles to define the world and claim its goods are carried out by unequally matched contestants, for certain social groups have historically controlled the ideologies, institutions and practices of their society, thereby maintaining their dominant position. But since these are socially and historically constructed, they can be reconstructed. One of the chief means of such re/construction is language. Therefore critical literacy critics and teachers focus on the cultural and ideological assumptions that underwrite texts, they investigate the politics of representation, and they interrogate the inequitable, cultural positioning of speakers and readers within discourses. They ask who constructs the texts whose representations are dominant in a particular culture at a particular time; how readers come to be complicit with the persuasive ideologies of texts; whose interests are served by such representations and such readings; and when such texts and readings are inequitable in their effects, how these could be constructed otherwise. They seek to promote the conditions for a different textual practice and therefore different political relations than present social, economic and political inequalities as these are generated and preserved by literacy practices within and beyond formal education.

3   Readers interested in assessing for themselves the contribution of this program to the learning of new literacies through new technologies will find some information at http://www.dse.vic.gov.au/cal_eval.htm which provides an executive summary and complete report commissioned by the Victorian Department of Education.

References

Bigum, C. and Green, B. (1993) 'Technologising literacy; or, interrupting the dream of reason', pp. 4–28 in A. Luke and P. Gilbert (eds), *Literacy in Context: Australian Perspectives and Issues*. Sydney: Allen and Unwin.

Bigum, C., Lankshear, C., *et al.* (1997) *Digital Rhetorics: Literacies and Technologies in Education – Current Practices and Future Directions*, Canberra: Department of Employment, Education, Training and Youth Affairs (Children's Literacy National Projects Program).

Green, B. (1988) 'Subject-specific literacy and school learning: A focus on writing', *Australian Journal of Education* 32, 2: 156–79.

Morgan, Wendy (1997) *Critical Literacy in the Classroom: The Art of the Possible*. London and New York: Routledge.

Ulmer, G. (1985) 'Textshop for Post(e)pedagogy', in G. Douglas Atkins and Michael L. Johnson (eds) *Writing and Reading Differently*. Kansas: University of Kansas Press.

7

New times! Old ways?

Colin Lankshear and Michele Knobel

Background

During recent years governments otherwise concerned with trimming public sector spending have often trumpeted 'funding packages' dedicated to improving 'literacy competence' among school-age and adult populations. Whenever such packages are announced, our own immediate response has increasingly been to wonder 'what does this package *really* mean so far as promoting a more literate and educated public is concerned?'

One of the authors recalls that during his final year of high school, in the context of a lesson on political reform in Britain, the history teacher made a link between three events and a political pronouncement. The events were the 1867 Reform Act (which extended the vote to some 1 million artisans living in the towns), the 1870 Education Act (which established a universal system of elementary schools for working-class children), and the 1884 Reform Act (which extended the vote to many 'unskilled' workers). The political pronouncement in question derived from Robert Lowe (Viscount Sherbrook), a champion of what became the 1870 Education Act. As interpreted by the history teacher, Lowe/Sherbrook was overtly advocating that a link be institutionalised between compulsory education, social control and economic interests. In other words: now that they are being given the vote, 'We must educate our masters.' The history teacher was, of course, far from alone in this interpretation. It has been almost a standard position among Marxist historians of British working-class education, notably Brian Simon (1960).

Lowe's views repay closer attention. In his letters and other written works, Lowe argued that since they were the majority of the voting population, working-class males would have the numerical potential to become:

> masters of the situation [with the power] to subvert the existing order of things, and to transfer power from the hands of property and intelligence, and so to place it in the hands of men whose whole life is necessarily occupied in the daily struggle for existence . . . . I believe it

will be absolutely necessary to compel our future masters to learn their letters.

(Martin, 1893, 262; Simon, 1960: 354)

[Once the men are given votes] the machinery is ready to launch those votes in one compact mass upon the institutions and property of this country.

At the same time, the higher classes would need 'superior education and superior cultivation', in order to 'know the things the working men know, only know them infinitely better in their principles and in their details'. By this means the higher classes could 'conquer back by means of a wider and more enlightened cultivation some of the influence which they have lost by political change' (Lowe, 1867: 8–10; Simon, 1960: 356).

Given the benefits of such historically informed hindsight, it makes good sense to begin from the assumption that compulsory mass schooling probably has a lot less to do with *educating* and *making literate* (in any truly expansive sense of these terms) than it has to do with producing other outcomes: outcomes which we should strive to make clear, and for which we should call governments, education officials, and teacher educators to account. We should train ourselves to recognise evidence for this assumption when we see it – which is often.

We will proceed from this assumption here and try to turn some everyday assumptions upside down. Our aim is to expose some anomalies and contradictions, and to assess some high profile trends apparent within literacy education at present against criteria that do not (in our view) figure sufficiently in public and political debate around education.

Two questions: Wayne O'Neil (1970)

In a powerful short polemic, 'Properly literate', Wayne O'Neil prompts us to rethink some 'common sense' assumptions about (il)literacy and disadvantage.

Who's Disadvantaged?

O'Neil says:

I have known but two illiterate adult Americans. . . . One was an ancient, a Mr Cole, North Carolina potter of a line of North Carolina-Staffordshire, English potters as far back as memory reaches. He runs a prospering pottery shop on Route 1 just outside Sanford, N.C. He finishes a firing every two weeks, everything gone long before the next firing is out of the kiln. People come in and order pots of all sizes and shapes and he has them write their orders in a fat, black book. Too bad.

He can't read. They never get their pots. So they learn to buy what he has or leave a picture behind and then get back before someone else buys it.
He does well.

(O'Neil, 1970: 261)

Who's Literate?

According to O'Neil:

In the tangled, demanding revolution that is America, if you're illiterate you have no control or at most you have only narrowly limited control. If you can only read and remain illiterate, you're worse off: you have no control.

Make a distinction: Being able to read means that you can follow words across a page, getting generally what's superficially there. Being literate means you can bring your knowledge and your experience to bear on what passes before you. Let us call the latter proper literacy; the former improper. You don't need to be able to read to be properly literate. Only in America and such like.

(ibid.: 261–2)

O'Neil believes children arrive at school properly literate relative to their experience, even though many (if not most) do not yet read and write. In teaching them to read and write, however, schools undermine and undo that proper literacy. The ways of school instruction displace bringing knowledge and experience to bear on what passes before one. In its place they impose the following of mere words – whose words?, which words? – across printed surfaces. O'Neil rejects this 'usurper literacy', calling it *improper*. This, however, is precisely what Robert Lowe wanted from mass schooling; an 'antidote' to the highly effective political organisation and agitation working people had engaged in throughout the nineteenth century. The organised political practices of the working classes were, indeed, grounded firmly in 'bringing knowledge and experience to bear on what passed before them' – every day.

There are good reasons for believing that, collectively, we are doing a pretty good job in education of keeping faith with the Viscount. Peter Freebody's (1992) account of what counts as being a successful reader, given the everyday demands of our cultural milieu, provides a good starting point for our argument.

Four roles as a literacy learner

Freebody argues that to become a successful reader an individual must 'develop and sustain the resources to play four related roles: code breaker, text-participant, text-user, and text-analyst' (1992: 48).

1 Code breaker: This is a matter of cracking alphabetic code/script – understanding the relationship between the twenty-six alphabetic written symbols and the forty-four sounds in English, and being able to move between sound and script in reading/decoding and writing/encoding.

2 Text-participant. This involves being able to handle the meaning and structure of texts, by bringing to the text itself the additional knowledge required for making meaning from that text – for example, knowledge of the topic, the kind of situation involved, the genre of the text, etc. Mere ability to decode is not sufficient for making meaning from a text: we can read plenty where we cannot understand, or that we understand differently from other successful decoders. Much depends on what we bring to the text with us. When we are faced with texts that we cannot bring much to, or where we cannot bring what others (who are deemed to comprehend better than we do) bring, we are disadvantaged by, or in relation to, that text and other readers.

3 Text-user: Successful reading requires ability to operate effectively and appropriately in text-mediated social activities. According to Freebody (1992: 53), being a successful text-user 'entails developing and maintaining resources for participating in "what this text is for, here and now"'. Reading, then, is a matter of matching texts to contexts, and knowing *how*, *what* and *why* to read and write within given contexts. It is what we sometimes refer to as getting the register or, perhaps, the genre 'right'. To foreshadow a theme we will return to later, Freebody comments that these resources 'are transmitted and developed in our society largely in instructional contexts, some of which may bear comparatively little relevance to the ways in which texts need to be used in out-of-school contexts' (ibid.).

4 Text-analyst: The reader as competent text-analyst is consciously aware that 'language and idea systems' are 'brought into play' whenever a text is constructed and, furthermore, that these systems are what 'make the text operate' and, thereby, make the reader, 'usually covertly, into its [i.e., the text's] operator' (ibid.: 56). Readers, in other words, become complicit in the work that texts do. This makes it very important to be aware of the need to interrogate texts, and to know how to interrogate them – since otherwise we may unwittingly participate in producing or maintaining effects we would not knowingly choose to. As basic examples of text interrogation, Freebody suggests asking 'What are the beliefs about the topic of a person who could utter this text?', and, 'What kind of person could unproblematically and acceptingly understand such a text?' This can be pushed further, by asking what kind of world – as lived contexts and sites which shape human identities and ways of being – do such and such texts sanction, promote, bolster and implicate us in making and maintaining?

Freebody concludes by insisting that these four roles not be seen as some kind of a sequence – developmental or otherwise. Rather, they are jointly necessary conditions for being a successful reader. Hence, they are necessary components of being a reader at each and every phase of our development and practice as readers. Whatever students' ages or developmental points, their reading programmes must promote and deal with each role in systematic and explicit ways (ibid.: 58).

Occupational hazards

From an account of guidelines to intervention strategies for reading and writing, Department of Education, Queensland, 1995a, we derive what we call two easy steps to improper literacy:

Two Easy Steps to Improper Literacy: Tread Carefully

Step 1

According to the guidelines:

> Our current beliefs about language learning lead us to understand that language is learned through using it, through talking about it and through seeing it in action in real contexts for real purposes.
>
> This is especially important for children who are experiencing some difficulties. They need to be able to experience language in real-life or lifelike contexts . . .
>
> Without meaningful and relevant contexts the less successful learners are trapped into reading, writing and speaking texts that are not natural and not related to the texts with which they are already familiar because of their life's experiences. (Department of Education, Queensland, 1995a: 7.)

Step 2

From the same guidelines, a few pages later:

> *Question*: What provision is made for ongoing one-to-one support for children's reading?
>
> *Answer*: The two recommended programmes are: Support-a-Reader and Reading Recovery. (ibid: 8)

Recovering what?

Let us take Reading Recovery as an example of a literacy intervention which is currently popular – and funded – in various parts of Britain, North America, Australia and New Zealand. Reading Recovery is a resource intensive intervention, enacted during the second year of schooling. It draws on the lowest performing 15–20 per cent of students in terms of reading achievement, and gives them up to six months – typically, twelve to twenty weeks – of individual instruction for a short period on a regular basis. The instruction is delivered by a Reading Recovery tutor, specially trained under the trademarked Reading Recovery regime, using Reading Recovery theory, resources and trainers. It is presented as an early detection/warning and prevention strategy. Its approach to diagnosis is based on a series of tasks and tests whereby student performance is documented as running records which observe the following dimensions – and which, thereby, define what reading *is* so far as the programme is concerned.

1 *Accuracy* – this is determined by keeping a running record of everything the child says or does as they read a book chosen by the RR teacher.
2 *Self-correction* – running records are kept by the RR teacher of self-correction by the child.
3 *Letter identification* – based on letters of the alphabet (randomly ordered and upper and lower case).
4 *Canberra word test* – correct responses to fifteen graded and often-used words are recorded.
5 *Concepts about print* – concepts that are tested include direction, text position, purposes of illustrations and visual patterns.
6 *Writing vocabulary* – the RR teacher records correctly spelled words from the 'bank' of words a child thinks s/he knows.
7 *Burt word reading test* – scores are calculated against an increasing order of difficulty.
8 *Dictation test* – provided by the RR teacher.

(cf. Trethowan *et al.*, 1996)

Each one-to-one tutorial session comprises a number of tasks, including reading familiar and unfamiliar texts from a set of carefully graded readers. The focus of these sessions is on enabling the students to comprehend 'messages' in the text (Department of Education, Queensland, 1996: 5), and running records of the relationship between what the text says and what the child reads are maintained by the tutor as the child is reading. One or two teaching points are selected from the running records as teaching foci for the tutorial session.

What happens when we look – as altogether too few commentators do – at Reading Recovery, and similar approaches, against the kind of model of successful reading proposed by Freebody? (It is worth keeping O'Neil's ideas in mind here as well.) What are children being apprenticed to in the name of literacy when they enter such programmes?

We suggest that they are being apprenticed to reading as the mechanics of code breaking, pure and simple. The Reading Recovery programme undoubtedly helps with code breaking but, other things being equal, we should not expect it to help with much else. Wherein lies a real danger. If taken seriously as any kind of panacea it is likely to divert attention from other areas of literacy education where, for many, learning is often less than the ideal dictates: notably, text-use and text-analysis. Interestingly, Marie Clay (1992) says that most graduates of Reading Recovery can return to classrooms and perform at average levels. From one perspective this is undoubtedly an achievement. From another, however, it may pose serious questions about what constitutes average performance – especially in relation to realistic notions of successful reading of the kind Freebody proffers, where the roles in question go far beyond code breaking.

On its own, approaches like Reading Recovery can make only a strictly limited contribution to resourcing these other roles, because they effectively reduce reading (these days referred to by their proponents as 'literacy') to the mechanics of breaking code. Larger aspects of participating in the text, let alone using and analysing texts, are simply not factored into the programme design. Whatever else 'recovering learners' get in the way of these wider elements of successful reading is left to the contingencies of their particular classroom teachers, their school programmes, and their wider life experiences (cf. Tancock, 1997). What is supposed to be an exemplary literacy intervention effectively bypasses three of our four necessary conditions for being a successful reader. Approaches like Reading Recovery appear to operate on the assumption: 'We will take care of code breaking. It's up to others to look after the rest.' This, however, fragments reading. It sends messages to learners that reading is code breaking. After all, if it were not, why would they be getting this special reading assistance on an individual basis? It would indeed be surprising if this message did not work against learners developing the richer conceptions and practices that literacy teachers are supposed to be enabling.

If we want learners to understand and practise reading in its fullness and richness, then that fullness and richness have to be there from the start, and in concert with each other as integral facets of any act of reading – as Freebody (1992: 58) notes. In this context we should recognise that it is, precisely, similar 'logics' of reductionism, compartmentalising and fragmentation (of literacy) that turn up at other points within schooling as, for example, 'keyboarding', masquerading as 'technological literacy', and in such ways reduce the use of electronic technologies to mere 'add ons' – rather than as an integrated part of three-dimensional social practices in which text production, distribution and exchange are organically embedded.

We find it interesting that the challenges and critiques we have seen addressed to Reading Recovery over the years by 'reading experts', and responded to by RR gurus, rarely come within a mile of having anything to do with analysing and using texts, or even *participating* in text, in Freebody's sense (cf. Clay, 1992). This is disturbing. The debate remains effectively at the level of whether and to what extent measured gains in code breaking can be attributed to the distinctiveness of Reading Recovery as a method, or whether some other method would do the job better (cf. Shanahan and Barr, 1995; Hiebert, 1996). This kind of debate simply reinforces the reduction of reading – let alone *literacy* – to code breaking. A fair analogy would be to say that learning to become a good driver is a matter simply of learning how to operate the vehicle's controls, and that the key issue is whether these operational skills are best acquired from Driving School A, Driving School B, or from a simulator.

Literacy validation

Further concerns arise when we turn to assessment and validation guidelines and practices such as those currently unfolding in a range of modern public education systems. In Queensland, for example, a Year 2 Diagnostic Net is being developed to catch and recover children 'who are experiencing difficulties in literacy and numeracy' (Department of Education, Queensland, 1995b: 1). Validation is one of four processes which collectively make up the Diagnostic Net. Teachers are to observe and map the progress of children in their classes using designated criteria. In validation, they verify (or disconfirm) these observations and maps using specially designed assessment tasks, and identify learners who need support. The other processes are providing literacy and numeracy learning support for the children identified as needing it, and reporting to parents.

Not surprisingly, we find further worrying traces of afflicted notions of literacy in such practices of validation. While the points sketched below warrant much deeper and more exacting investigation than can be provided here, we believe literacy educators and curriculum and policy developers should pay such matters very close attention. Readers are encouraged to make their own local adjustments to the examples which follow.

The four texts identified for use as validation instruments in Queensland in 1996 were themselves highly problematic (Department of Education Queensland, 1995b). They were: *My Grandma*, by Sarah Keane; *Mrs Goose's Baby*, by Charlotte Voake; *Fancy That*, by Pamela Allen; and *Some Snakes*, by Kathleen Murdoch and Stephen Ray. (Equivalent texts were chosen for 1997: cf. *The Elephant Tree*, by Penny Dale; *Walk through the Jungle*, by Julie Lacome; *Ants*, by Ron Thomas and Jan Stutchbury). The problem is not so much with the books in and of themselves, but rather that they represent a very narrow range of texts and text types, reflect an unacceptably narrow range of textual purposes (effectively reducing young learners as language users to the status of consumers of stories), and, for many children in the target range, are highly unlikely to comprise authentic texts. An obvious point of comparison so far as promoting and assessing competence around authentic language purposes are concerned can be found, for instance, in the work of teachers described by Shirley Heath in *Ways with Words* (1983). Progressive and useful assessment purposes would be far better served by employing richer and more 'authentic' texts. This, of course, is to say nothing of wider concerns about the particular discourse of assessing (testing) inherent in the validation exercise described here. In fact, the very *criteria* for text selection – readability, literary quality and the extent to which they satisfy social justice criteria – are problematic in this particular case. The social justice criterion, while a very important principle in its own right, is undermined by the texts chosen. Readability and literary quality can be seen to be inadequate in terms of acceptable notions of what counts as successful reading.

The notion of *contextualising* involved in the teaching and validation process appears to be at odds with promoting serious text participation (cf. Freebody, 1992). The point about text participation is that meaning will be made more effectively where readers bring lived forms of experience and knowledge to bear on a text. The suggestions provided for contextualisation activities around the texts build on problematic constructions of children as readers. Once again, if we take, for example, the activities suggested for working with *Mrs Goose's Baby*, and compare these with the modes of contextualisation enacted by Heath's exemplar teachers, the point becomes quite clear (cf. Department of Education, Queensland, 1995b: 41–43; Heath, 1983).

The text-user resourcing potential of such texts is limited inherently and in terms of range. How, exactly, might learners be enhanced as text-*users* within the parameters of these texts and the construction of reading as social practice they invite?

Much the same point holds for resourcing the role of text-*analyst* – although the problem here has less to do with the choice of texts than with the fact that the validation process seemingly has no concern whatsoever for this role.

As it happens, the kind of assessment in question is perfectly coherent and appropriate given what is envisaged as subsequent *support*. In terms of the ideas and values integral to a defensible concept of successful reading, however, the nature of that support, and its underlying 'philosophy', is highly problematic.

Tape recorders as tools for literacy

The sorts of issues we have been trying to get at so far can be neatly illustrated by reference to two very different approaches to using tape recorders in literacy enhancement activities. One approach is outlined in *Intervention Strategies: Reading and Writing* (Department of Education, Queensland,

1995a). Here the tape recorder is used in conjunction with written texts as an aid to helping readers identify words and follow the text – i.e., break the code – and, perhaps – to get better access to the meaning of a text they might otherwise find difficult to make meaningful. The procedure is augmented by use of oral cloze exercises, where the person making the tape leaves a generous pause so that the learner can fill in the gap.

A very different approach is evident in the rich examples provided by Heath (1983; see also Heath and Mangiola, 1991). Heath describes tape recorders being used by teachers and learners to tape real-life transactions, conversations, and participation in other literacy events – such as constructing narratives and other generic forms. These are then exchanged – at times among different year levels and different schools (from different kinds of community) – and used as opportunities for making differences in kind and quality among various texts explicit; for editing purposes; for accessing different cultures; and for expanding the range of text types over which learners gain mastery. In one example, Heath (1983: 297–8) reports how a previously low achieving African American child learned to produce written stories which obeyed the conventions of mainstream print narratives through a process of 'augmenting' tape-recorded oral texts, thereby accessing modes of school discourse which are more highly rewarded than those she had available to her via her 'primary discourse' (Gee *et al.*, 1996). Over a two-year period this child moved from being a very low performer to acting as editor of collaborative text productions. In other cases, teachers who transcribed their students' recorded oral stories found some children rejecting these oral versions upon seeing them in print, and developing new sensitivities to the kinds of accounts other classmates liked to read (and why). In such cases we find rich and real approximations to the kinds of outcomes Freebody sees as integral to successful reading. We also find learners attaining the kinds of 'higher order literacy' outcomes espoused in a range of education reform statements: outcomes which are put at risk by emergent narrow and one-dimensional regimes of assessment and validation. Not surprisingly, reports of teachers teaching to the validation tests from Year 1 began to surface in Queensland shortly after literacy validation was announced. This is a perfectly understandable and predictable response on the part of 'accountable teachers'. It is, however, bad news for successful reading.

How do we get out of such messes? One way is by paying less homage to psychology-based approaches to reading, and directing greater attention instead to what James Gee calls 'a sociocultural approach to literacies'.

A sociocultural approach to literacies[1]

When we take a sociocultural approach to literacy we turn our attention from the mind and, ultimately, the school, and enter instead the *world*, including the adult world of work. From a sociocultural approach, the focus of learning and education is not *children*, nor *schools*, but, rather, *human lives* as *trajectories* through multiple *social practices* in various social institutions. If learning is to be efficacious, then what a child or adult does *now* as a 'learner' must be connected in meaningful and motivating ways with 'mature' ('insider') versions of related social practices.

The focus of education should be on *social practices* and their connections across various social and cultural sites and institutions. Learners should be viewed as life-long *trajectories* through these sites and institutions, as *stories* with multiple twists and turns. What we say about their beginnings should be shaped by what we intend to say about their middles and ends, and vice-versa. As *their* stories are rapidly and radically changing, we need to change *our* stories about skills, learning, and knowledge. Our focus, as well, should be on multiple learning sites and their rich and complex interconnections.

If learning is not to be a senseless activity (which, regrettably it sometimes is), it is always about entry into and participation in a Discourse.[2] Unfortunately, a focus on children and schooling tends to obscure the role of social practices and Discourses. Some Discourses, like law, have a separate domain for (initial) initiation into the Discourse (namely, law school). Others, including many Discourses connected to workplaces, do not engage in such a separation to any such extent. In these cases, much learning and initiation into the Discourse occurs 'on the job'. In both cases, however, the connection between learning and participation in the 'mature' Discourse (law or work) is relatively clear. The same is true of family, community and public sphere-based Discourses.

School-based Discourses are quite anomalous in this respect. Schools don't merely separate learning from participation in 'mature' Discourses: they actually render the connections entirely mysterious (as we will see in some cases provided below). Schools and classrooms most certainly create Discourses, that is, they create social practices that integrate people, deeds, values, beliefs, words, tools, objects and places. They create, as well, social positions (identities) for kinds of students and teachers. However, the Discourse of the school or classroom is primarily a Discourse devoted to learning – but, learning for *what*? Is it learning for participation in the school or classroom Discourse itself, or learning for Discourses outside school? Which Discourses outside of school? And what sort of relationship to these outside Discourses should (or do) school and classroom Discourses contract?

These are complex questions and issues. The separation between school-based Discourses and 'outside' Discourses may be a good thing, or it may not be. It all depends on how we answer such questions as 'What is the point (goal, purpose, vision) of school-based Discourses?' 'What is the point (goal, purpose, vision) of this or that specific school-based Discourse (e.g., elementary school reading or secondary school English)?' What we *can* say, without much doubt, is that turning school Discourses of literacy into so many intervention programmes that undermine apprenticeship to 'mature' versions of social practices does no one much good in the long run. Neither does turning literacy into distinctively *school* Discourses. For evidence of this, let us turn, finally, to some real-life cases from local research.

Right now we are at an important literacy conjuncture. New literacy practices are emerging around new technologies which are making ever deeper incursions into everyday social practices, spanning the range from leisure to work, via communications, business, trade, etc. These changes have major implications for literacy learning, forcing us to consider what is involved in being a text-participant, text-user, and text-analyst in 'new times'. The cases which follow are intended to provide some insights into how different learners and teachers are negotiating the present conjuncture. They are based on fieldwork done in Queensland school, home and community settings (cf. Knobel, 1997), and have been further described in other publications (see Knobel, 1996; Lankshear and Knobel, 1996a, 1996b, 1997).

A case in point

Jacques (thirteen years) was a Year 7 student in a large state primary school. His teacher described him as experiencing much difficulty with literacy at school. He belongs to a self-employed single-income family. Jacques' father runs an earth-moving business, while his mother administers the home and is heavily involved in volunteer church work. The family lives in a predominantly white executive neighbourhood.

There was no computer in Jacques' classroom. His teacher lamented 'poor decision-making' (prior to the time she began working at the school) which established a computing lab stocked with little-known machines for which no up-to-date software was available, and which broke down regularly, requiring costly and time-consuming repairs. She had given up trying to use them. All but three of her thirty students had computer access at home, and she occasionally set word-processing tasks for homework.

Jacques loathed school, and was patiently 'doing time' until he could leave in Year 10 and work with his father. He found the world of adult work far more compelling than school. He insisted he was 'not a pen man', and could not see any point in going to school. During class, Jacques would engineer elaborate strategies and ruses for evading school work, particularly where there was any writing involved. Indeed, his teacher bemoaned his treatment of the Writers' Centre, in the corner of the classroom, where Jacques had recently spent two hours stapling together a miniature blank leafed book on which he subsequently wrote a narrative comprising two or three words per page – effectively 'sending up' the process writing approach adopted in this classroom.

There was a computer at home, which was mainly used by Jacques' father for keeping records and accounts. Jacques, too, used it for business purposes. With some editorial help from his mother and brother, he designed and published a flier advertising 'JP's Mowing Service'. The flier, complete with a carefully produced graphic, was exemplary in its business-like language and practices: 'efficient reliable service', 'all edging done', and 'for free quote phone . . . ' It was printed, photocopied and dropped in neighbourhood letterboxes, and Jacques had soon established a thriving mowing business over the summer holidays.

This 'snapshot' juxtaposes Jacques' home literacy practice against his classroom practice. At home he integrates a computer into a discourse to which he has been apprenticed and with which he feels an affinity. This is a business discourse, which was certainly marginal to the point of being invisible in class during the period of data collection, yet which is a powerful discourse so far as adult life is concerned. The technology-mediated literacy which Jacques engaged at home, despite the fact that he finds typing laborious, is likewise a potentially powerful literacy, assuming an enterprise (sub)culture. This contrasts markedly with his response to school literacy practices where, if computers were employed, he would likely reject them in the same way that he rejected the technologies (pen and paper) of conventional print.

'What a child does now as a "learner" must be connected in meaningful and motivating ways with "mature" ("insider") versions of related social practices': A case in point

Like Jacques, Layla was a Year 7 student in 1995. Although there was a computer in her classroom it was not used during the two-week research observation period. The Year 7 class next door, however, had a computer with a modem connection, and Layla was observed using this computer during a session intended to introduce students formally to e-mail. During the first e-mail session the task was for the group to collect and decipher a cryptic clue sent by another school as their first step in making their way around Australia to track down a (virtual) criminal. In subsequent sessions they used e-mail to send and gain further clues about the gradually unfolding trail mapped out for each participating school by headquarters. Students used an atlas and did other research work in the course of composing their cryptic e-mail messages and deciphering clues that were in turn sent to them.

The teacher pointed to a list of instructions he had written on sheets of paper that morning and stuck to the wall above the computer terminal. He talked the students through each step, instructing Layla what to key in, as the others looked on, increasingly offering advice or corrections. At times

Layla hesitated or looked confused, until someone helped her out, then she laughed and continued on. The teacher explained passwords and user-names, sending and receiving mail, organising mailboxes, session menus, file capturing, creating files, scroll bars, the mouse, printing in 'economy' mode, and closing down connections, all the while reminding the group that they needed to work quickly because 'time is money'. The telephone line was shared with the school administration, and the students were told that administrative staff 'always had right of way' on this line. The log-on process was repeated, this time with a different keyboarder. The teacher talked about 'agreeing to pretend' they were detectives following a trail of clues, using non-sexist language in their messages, and about managing information.

The students opened their electronic mailbox and found their first clue: 'Criminal was overheard talking about travelling north to gamble.' They began discussing possible answers, then moved to tables to look through descriptions sent in earlier by participating schools and downloaded that morning by the teacher. At different times they used atlases to check a 'suspected' school's location. Everybody made notes as they went, and discussed possibilities with each other, before finally agreeing that the message referred to a school in Townsville (where there is a casino). Using pen and paper, they drafted an e-mail message or, as the teacher called it, 'a letter'. The group logged-on again, and keyed in their edited letter. The teacher demonstrated how to send messages, and drew their attention again to the instructions pinned to the wall.

During the next four weeks this group logged in and checked their mailbox during non-lesson times (e.g., before school, lunchtime, etc.), decoded clues, and passed on information to other participating schools. None of this work was otherwise linked to classroom work or events. Layla said she enjoyed participating, although she didn't quite understand why she was doing it, or how it all worked.

While schools are coming under increasing pressure to introduce new technologies into their curriculum, teachers are very often poorly prepared for doing this in any integrated way. Often, the result is just one more 'add on'. Students engage in established learning activities, except that computers are added on – as, for example, where students write a narrative and then key it in using a computer and a word processing package. While this contributes to students acquiring keyboard skills and, perhaps, operating spell and grammar checkers, it does not constitute an initiation into full-fledged forms of computer-mediated composition and communication. Entirely new social practices with their characteristic embedded languages and literacies are emerging apace around new technologies. Many of these are tomorrow's powerful literacies: for example, web pages as commercial advertising and information ventures, 'infotainment' or 'infomercial' genres, conducting business by e-mail, etc.

Effective integration of new technologies into worthwhile and engaging forms of learning presupposes theoretical finesse and knowledge of authentic social practices associated with these technologies, which many teachers currently lack. Mastery, fruitful experimentation, testing the borders of extant practices, inventing new social practices and technology-mediated literacies, and so on, call for knowledge, relevant experience, and a good theoretical grasp of 'authentic' practices – i.e., practices as they occur in the world, and practices *that* occur in the world. The necessary theoretical grasp and knowledge of authentic social practices in which new technologies are embedded cannot be acquired merely by means of 'quick fix' inservice and professional development packages. While such provisions assist teachers to get on top of changing literacy demands and new ways of meeting them, we need to dig deep into teacher education, bringing the best of theory together with the best of practice, so that the teachers who go into classrooms are properly prepared for understanding the worlds from which their students come and the worlds to which they will go, and for knowing how to act pedagogically on that understanding.

Even though a range of technology-mediated literacy practices operated in the Year 7 classrooms on which the 'snapshots' of Jacques and Layla are based (as well as others in the same study), they were typically of an 'add-on' nature. When potential opportunities arose to use technologies in 'real-world' ways within classrooms – such as e-mail, which has become an organic part of academic and economic production in many countries – they were reduced to 'school' exercises: militating against students making ready links between what they were learning in the way of technological literacies at school, and what they might need in their (future) lives beyond school.[3]

On being advantaged in acquiring and learning new literacies

Alex is five years old. He began school recently. He reads and writes conventional texts, but much of his text production is computer mediated. Alex has his own web site, *Koala Trouble*, which he produces with the assistance of his father, Scott. Alex creates the images for stories featuring Max, a young koala bear. Several Max stories have now been published on the site, with more in process. All employ a simple hypertext format, with instructions (typically in the form of clues or questions) about where to click to move to the next page. Alex produces the drawings by hand as a story sequence in the manner of a story board and, with help from Scott, scans them into a PC and colours them using a paintbox program, 'Animator Pro'. The page includes a feedback link enlisting active involvement of other children from around the world. Their collaboration takes two main forms. Many send e-mail messages to Alex's page responding to the stories. Others (also) 'host' Max on his new 'round the world trip' – by sending back to Alex and Scott pictures, stories and ideas about Max visiting and having adventures in their part of the world, to be added to the page.

The idea behind this site is to promote cooperative activity by children who are stimulated by material designed and drawn by their peers (beginning with Alex): a global classroom as seen through the eyes of children, based on information delivered by children for children in a format they can relate to. Alex is described by Scott as 'a mean Net surfer' who finds most of the material on the Net 'boring' – hence the Koala trouble web, 'a page for kids (of all ages)'. Alex's page registered more than 60,000 'hits' – national and international – during January and February 1996. Among the accolades for *Koala Trouble* are included an 'awesome page' rating from *Kids on the Net* author, Brendan Kehoe, a 'must see' rating from *Yahoo*, and a 'wonderful' from *Berit's Best Children Sites*. Alex replies personally to all his e-mail, often by typing 'Alex', leaving the message to Scott, and hitting the Send button. With so many messages to reply to, there is a risk – which Scott is keen to avoid – of Alex becoming bored with and alienated from the medium. At five, there are other things to do!

Scott completed Year 12 at age fifteen, but never went on to tertiary education. He began a computer-based marketing industry in his tool shed in 1990, and by 1994 had formed four companies involved in all areas of multimedia (touch screen kiosks to floppy-disk-based presentations). His clients have included some major national, international, and multinational companies in areas as diverse as air transportation, banking and newspapers, as well as government departments. After doing a computer-based presentation of his 'vision for the electronic community of the future' to a city council in Queensland, Scott was contracted to set up that city's electronic network. At the end of his contract, Scott established Global Web Builders (GWB), a company which builds commercial webs for clients. GWB's home page is called *The Definitive Lifestyle Guide to Australian Webs* (DLG), and is found at http://www.gwb.com.au/gwb /guide.html. It attracts an enormous amount of global traffic and is today the Australian gateway on the Internet, registering more than 360,000 national and international hits in the week 5–12 February 1996.

The DLG concept is now being franchised globally through a multinational company called GLOBE (Global Online Business Enterprises) International. GLOBE International have sites in New Zealand and are in the process of signing up GLOBE Asia with 9 Asian countries participating. *Koala Trouble* is a specific niche market on the DLG – (i.e., families and kids): one of a number of niche market content-based webs generating traffic for the DLG.

Scott laments the fact that at school 'they play silly games on computers', adding 'that's fine for a start', but maximum use of the Internet 'within a controlled project-based environment must be part of the very early curriculum' if children's education for life in the information age is not to be stunted. According to Scott, Alex's *Koala Trouble* page is much more than just a web: 'it's a major educational "lifestyle" opportunity for Alex', comprising the hub of an electronic community of Internet users who receive monthly e-mail newsletters on what's up at *Koala Trouble*, and who reciprocate with e-mail correspondence – much of it from school classes in the US.

The company was approached by the Australian Koala Foundation (AKF) and the two have collaborated to produce a line of T-Shirts which carry Alex's pictures of Max as well as the Alex's Scribbles URL. Sale of the T-Shirts provides funds for the AKF, and Alex's Scribbles receives a share of the profits. 'With our e-mail list we have a ready market and credibility through the AKF. Alex at five has a business. I registered Alex's Scribbles last week. I (on Alex's behalf) have entered into preliminary arrangements on a profit share of the Koala Trouble T-Shirt' (Scott in e-mail interview 29 February 1996). Looking beyond schooling toward Alex's education for his later years, Scott emphasises the relevance of the discursive logic which is integral to their joint activity: namely, 'global contacts, global perspective, product line, business based on his (i.e., Alex's) work, and new opportunities as he embraces the technology' (e-mail interview, 29 February 1996). The joint venture was launched publicly on 19 April 1996. Alex performed his part well.

Whatever we may think of such social practices and the literacies they 'house', there is no question that what Alex is acquiring and learning at the age of five has everything to do with be(com)ing 'connected' in meaningful, motivating and motivated ways with mature versions of related authentic social practices. What is at issue here is more the principle(s) evinced by the case than the specific nature and detail of the social practice itself. The point is that if we are to promote equal or better literacy learning in the times that lie ahead as we have managed in the present and the recent past, we will need to come to terms with what constitutes successful *reading* in these times, and observe the importance of establishing meaningful and motivating links between what learners learn now and what they will encounter as 'the real thing'. These three cases provide the basis for a perspective on this claim.

A larger frame on 'mature' social practices

What *is* the adult world of social practices that students like Jacques, Layla, and Alex are moving toward? What are the 'mature' versions of social practices they are likely to encounter? By way of working toward an end point, let us address some aspects of the adult world of work they seem destined to face. There are many other dimensions of their future worlds that merit mention, such as the nature of effective and engaged citizenship, parenthood, the global world, and so on. In this chapter we will look solely at work, not least because this provides an important basis from which to reflect on other dimensions. It also intimates the importance of developing and, by means of meaningful and motivating links, apprenticing learners to mature versions of critically literate practices: practices which are integral to Freebody's account of successful reading.

In *The Work of Nations* (1992), Robert Reich argues that three broad categories of work are emerging across nations within the new world economy. He calls these 'routine production services', 'in-person services', and 'symbolic-analytic services' respectively. Between them they will eventually account for almost all the paid work performed in modern economies. While the percentages in the first two categories are continuing to grow, the proportion of symbolic-analytic workers in the US workforce has become more or less static.

Symbolic-analytic work involves services which are delivered in the forms of data, words, and oral and visual representations. It comprises diverse problem-identifying, problem-solving, and strategic brokering activities (Reich, 1992: 177). As such, symbolic-analytic services span the work of research scientists, all manner of engineers (from civil to sound), management consultants, investment bankers, systems analysts, authors, editors, art directors, video and film producers, musicians, and so on.

Unlike symbolic-analytic work, much of the work within the first two categories is not seen as substantial value-adding activity. Furthermore, beyond demands for basic numeracy and the ability to read, such work often calls primarily for reliability, loyalty and the capacity to take direction, and, in the case of in-person service workers, 'a pleasant demeanour'. Thus, there is a vast potential labour pool which is now global. The logistics of labor supply and demand, in conjunction with the perceived low value-additive nature of this work, mean that such work is poorly rewarded relative to symbolic-analytic work.

Against this backdrop, Reich speaks of a rising one-fifth and a falling four-fifths within the new work order of economies like our own.

> By highlighting different categories and 'realities' of work, which are either ignored or are at best glossed over by most authors and texts, Reich's account indicates a potential – and increasingly actual – problem of alarming depth and proportions for modern economies. . . . The lean and mean hyper-competitive perfection-driven nature of contemporary capitalism requires a core of relatively well paid knowledge leaders and workers supplemented by a bevy of people 'servicing' them for the least possible price so that their ideas can be translated into the highest quality, most competitive products possible. These 'servants', whether in a less developed country or in Third World pockets of 'developed' countries, will 'merit' their lowly

places because of their lack of knowledge and education – the new currency of the new capitalism.

(Gee, Hull and Lankshear, 1996: 47)

This, of course, brings us back to Viscount Sherbrook/Robert Lowe. According to Peter Drucker, who is no political radical by any stretch of the imagination, the social challenge of the post-capitalist society will, be the dignity of the second class in (what he calls, intriguingly) 'post-capitalist society': the service workers. Service workers, as a rule, says Drucker, lack the necessary education to be knowledge workers. And in every country, even the most highly advanced one, they will constitute the majority (Drucker, 1993: 8; ibid.).

Reich sees no easy way out of this. The one recommendation he advances is to invest in promoting the wealth-creating capacities of our compatriots: in a way, to turn them all into value adders, in the kind of way Scott and Alex have been able to add value to particular 'new' literacies. This, unfortunately, cannot work. In fact, so far as conventional understandings of the ideal are concerned, educational reform based on ensuring 'quality' schools for everyone is deeply paradoxical. Clearly, if *everyone* were educated there would be no one to do the *serving*. The new capitalism of the global information economy is in danger of producing and reproducing an even steeper pyramid than the old capitalism of the industrial era. And, just as in the old capitalism, it will need institutions – like schools, first and foremost – to reproduce that social structure (Gee, Hull and Lankshear, 1996: 47).

Reich suggests that on the basis of recent and current trends, the futures of the best and worst off in economies like our own will continue to diverge to the extent that, unless appropriate interventions are enacted, by the year 2020 'the top fifth of American earners will account for more than 60 per cent of all the income earned by Americans; the bottom fifth 2 per cent' (Reich 1992: 302). Reich develops an even deeper dimension to this problem:

America's problem is that while some Americans are adding substantial value, most are not. In consequence, the gap between those few in the first group and everyone else is widening. To improve the economic position of the bottom four-fifths will require that the fortunate fifth share its wealth and invest in the wealth-creating capacities of other Americans. Yet as the top becomes ever more tightly linked to the global economy, it has less stake in the performance and potential of its less fortunate compatriots. Thus our emerging dilemma, and that of other nations as well.

(ibid.: 301)

Critical social literacy as a millennium literacy

There are some ironies here. First, if we accept that education is about preparing people for the society they will enter, what we are currently doing in the way of literacy education may work just fine – as it has since the time of Robert Lowe. We can continue to develop and even enhance the capacity of people to break codes, participate in text-mediated social practices, and use the normal range of texts – and take our chances on the shrinking range of pathways to viable and dignified futures, and all that goes with it: from escalating views among youth that there is no future; escalating rates of youth suicide; and escalating enactments of desperation. If nothing else, that may create jobs in property-guarding and personal security and the like. Schools can continue to generate established patterns of 'success' and 'failure', and to legitimate these through school Discourses and forms of assessment that deliver up league tables of 'good' schools and 'bad' schools, and that continue to generate interventions that focus on enhanced code breaking performances that are effectively roads to nowhere – or nowhere much. Equally, we can place our faith in high-tech classrooms that permit similar outcomes to be achieved with still larger class sizes – albeit with more alienating work conditions and lower remuneration rates for teachers, together with continuing experience of being blamed for the alleged consequences of a failing school system.

Alternatively, we can embrace a second irony: namely, that the literacies we need for the new millennium contain elements that have been practised and refined for thousands of years – as well as containing elements that are distinctively new. The call to interrogate texts critically in search of the good life is, in the Western tradition, at least as old as Socrates; and in other traditions as old if not older again. The call to create and engage texts which search for ways of actualising humanity on just and reciprocal bases is absolutely fundamental and binding to the 'post-everything' age. What we need to do as literacy educators is to reinvent textual practices that enable us to bring our knowledge and experience to bear on what passes before us, filtered through an ideal of lives of dignity and fulfilment for all, and grounded in a conviction that a world in which this ideal is possible remains open to people prepared to collaborate in building it. This is much more than a matter of being able to 'follow words across a page [or a screen], getting generally what's superficially there' – although for some time to come it will probably *include* the capacity to decode and encode print.

We do well to remember this when we look at multimillion dollar budget breaks for literacy. And we do well to remember also that much of what we need to consider is *already* available to us. It is, for example, available in concepts like C. Wright Mills' notion of 'sociological imagination' (Mills, 1959), when suitably reworked to take account of recent developments in social, ethical and epistemological theories advanced in response to distinctive conditions of lived experience in new times. It is also, we venture, available in a sociocultural approach to literacy which insists that language and literacy must always be understood in their social, cultural and political contexts. One of these contexts is the globally interconnected space of the new global economy, with its new competition and its new work order, *and in all its ramifications*. For

> language – indeed, our very humanity – is in danger of losing meaning if we do not carefully reflect on this context and its attempts to make us into 'new kinds' of people . . . e.g., people who are 'smart' because they [produce and] buy the highest 'quality' [with the greatest efficiency, accountability, and cost effectiveness], but do not care about – or even see – the legacies of their greed writ large on the world.
>
> (Gee, Hull and Lankshear, 1996: 150–151)

Endword

In the end, we have more to recover than our *reading*, although we have *that* to recover as well: albeit in a much more generous and expansive sense than many of our current practices admit – including some of those most in favour among politicians and administrators at present.

Notes

1   This section draws directly on Gee, Hull and Lankshear, 1996: 4, 6, 15–16.
2   In what follows we observe James Paul Gee's distinction between 'Discourse' and 'discourse'. For Gee, a Discourse is a 'socially accepted association among ways of using language, other symbolic expressions, and artifacts, of thinking, feeling, believing, valuing and acting that can be used to identify us as a member of a socially meaningful group' (Gee, 1991: 131). Gee uses 'discourse' to refer to the 'language bits' in Discourses: that is, connected stretches of language that make sense within some Discourse community or other (e.g., a report within a research Discourse), an essay within a scholastic Discourse.
3   This section is based on material previously published in Lankshear and Knobel, 1996a, 1996b, 1997.

References

Balson, A. and Balson, S. (1996) 'Alex's scribbles – Koala trouble' http://www.scribbles.com.au
Balson, S./Global Web Builders (1996) 'Definitive lifestyle guide to Australian webs' http://www..gwb.com.au/gwb/guide.html
Clay, M. (1992) 'Reading Recovery: The wider implications of an educational innovation'. In A. Watson and A. Badenhop (eds) *Prevention of Reading Failure*. Sydney: Ashton Scholastic, 22–47.

Department of Education, Queensland (1995a) *Intervention Strategies: Reading and Writing*. Brisbane: Department of Education.

Department of Education, Queensland (1995b) *Literacy Validation*. Brisbane: Department of Education.

Department of Education, Queensland (1996) *Reading Recovery Queensland: Information Package for Schools 1996*. Brisbane: Department of Education (mimeo).

Drucker, P. (1993) *Post-Capitalist Society*. New York: Harper Books.

Freebody, P. (1992) 'A socio-cultural approach: resourcing four roles as a literacy learner'. In A. Watson and A. Badenhop (eds) *Prevention of Reading Failure*. Sydney: Ashton Scholastic, 48–60.

Gee, J. P. (1991) 'What is literacy?' In C. Mitchell and K. Weiler (eds) *Rewriting Literacy*. New York: Bergin and Garvey, 1–11.

—— (1992) *Social Linguistics and Literacies: Ideology in Discourses*, second edition. London: Taylor and Francis.

Gee, J. P., Hull, G. and Lankshear, C. (1996) *The New Work Order: Behind the Language of the New Capitalism*. Sydney and Boulder CO.: Allen and Unwin and Westview Press.

Heath, S. B. (1983) *Ways with Words: Language, Life and Work in Communities and Classrooms*. Cambridge: Cambridge University Press.

Heath, S. B. and Mangiola, L. (1991) *Children of Promise: Literate Activity in Linguistically and Culturally Diverse Classrooms*. Washington, DC: National Education Association of the United States.

Hiebert, M. (1996) 'Revisiting the question: what difference does Reading Recovery make to an age cohort?' in *Educational Researcher* 25 (7): 26–8.

Jones, C. (May 16 1996) 'Big boosts for literacy and health programs'. *The Australian*, p. 5.

Knobel, M. (1996) 'Language and social purposes in adolescents' everyday lives'. *Australian Journal of Language and Literacy* 19 (2): 120–8.

—— (1997) 'Language and social practices in the everyday lives of four adolescents.' Unpublished Ph.D. thesis. Brisbane: Faculty of Education, QUT.

Lankshear, C. and Knobel, M. (1996a) 'Different worlds' http://www.fed.qut.edu.au/crn/index.html

—— (1996b) 'Different worlds: technology-mediated classroom learning and students' social practices with new technologies in home and community settings'. Symposium presentation to American Educational Research Association Annual Conference, April. New York: AERA.

—— (1997) 'Different worlds: new technologies in school, home and community' in C. Lankshear, *Changing Literacies*. Buckinghamshire: Open University Press.

Lowe, R. (1867) 'Primary and classical education'. Cited in Simon, 1960.

Martin, A. Patchett (1893) *Life and Letters of the Right Honourable Robert Lowe Viscount Sherbrook*. Vol II. Cited in Simon, 1960.

Mills, C. Wright (1959) *The Sociological Imagination*. New York: Oxford University Press.

O'Neil, W. (1970) 'Properly literate'. *Harvard Educational Review* 40 (2): 260–3.

Reich, R. (1992) *The Work of Nations*. New York: Vintage Books.

Shanahan, T. and Barr, R. (1995) 'Reading Recovery: an independent evaluation of the effects of an early instructional intervention for at-risk learners'. *Reading Research Quarterly* 50 (4): 958–96.

Simon, B. (1960) *Studies in the History of Education 1780–1870*. London: Lawrence and Wishart.

Tancock, S. (1997) 'Catie: a case study of one first grader's reading status'. *Reading Research and Instruction* 36 (2): 89–110.

Trethowan, V., Harvey, D. and Fraser, C. (1996) 'Reading Recovery: Comparison between its efficacy and normal classroom instruction'. *Australian Journal of Language and Literacy* 19 (1): 29–36.

Index